From America with Love

CLASSICS OF CARPATHO-RUSYN SCHOLARSHIP

Published under the auspices of the Carpatho-Rusyn Research Center
Patricia A. Krafcik and Paul Robert Magocsi, editors

Mary Halász

From America with Love
Memoirs of an American Immigrant in the Soviet Union

Written together with
Piroska É. Kiss and Katalin É. Kiss

With an introduction by
István Deák

EAST EUROPEAN MONOGRAPHS
Distributed by Columbia University Press, New York

2000

EAST EUROPEAN MONOGRAPHS, No. DLXIV

Composition and layout by Gabriele Scardellato.

ISBN 0-88033-462-2
Library of Congress Catalog Card Number 00-132347

Series Preface

The series entitled Classics of Carpatho-Rusyn Scholarship is a publication project of the Carpatho-Rusyn Research Center that is intended to make available in English translation some of the best monographs dealing with Carpatho-Rusyn culture. These monographs deal with several scholarly disciplines: history, language, literature, ethnography, folklore, religion, music, and archaeology.

Many of the studies included in this series were first published during the twentieth century and were written in various languages by authors who may have had definite attitudes and preferences regarding the national and political orientations of the indigenous Carpatho-Rusyn population. Such preferences are often revealed in the varied terminology used to describe the group—Carpatho-Ruthenians, Carpatho-Russians, Carpatho-Ukrainians, Lemkos, Ruthenes, Ruthenians, Rusyns, etc. In keeping with the policy of the Carpatho-Rusyn Research Center, the inhabitants and culture which are the subject of this series will be referred to consistently as Carpatho-Rusyn or Rusyn, regardless what term or terms may have been used in the original work.

The appearance in this series of scholarly monographs whose authors may favor a particular national (pro-Russian, pro-Rusyn, pro-Ukrainian), political (pro-Czechoslovak, pro-Hungarian, pro-Soviet), or ideological (pro-democratic, pro-Communist, pro-Christian) stance does not in any way reflect the policy or orientation of the Carpatho-Rusyn Research Center. Rather it is felt that the availability in English of scholarly studies representing a variety of ideological persuasions is the best way to improve our understanding and appreciation of Carpatho-Rusyn culture.

As in other publications of the Carpatho-Rusyn Research Center, placenames are rendered according to the official language used in the country where they are presently located; therefore, Slovak in Slovakia;

Ukrainian in the Transcarpathian oblast of Ukraine; Polish in the Lemko Region of Poland; and Serbo-Croatian in the Vojvodina (Bačka) of Yugoslavia. Either the Library of Congress or the international transliteration system is used to render words and names from the Cyrillic alphabet.

This volume differs from others in our series in that it is not a scholarly monograph, but rather a personal memoir that reflects a somewhat unique phenomenon: the life of an American "immigrant" in the Soviet Union. It is, moreover, one of the few sources in any language that provides an insight into daily life under Soviet rule during the height of Stalinism just after World War II. For these reasons, this volume is a worthy addition to the Classics in Carpatho-Rusyn Scholarship series.

Patricia A. Krafcik
Paul Robert Magocsi
March 2000

Contents

Introduction

I t may have been a year ago that I received the manuscript of Mary Halász's memoirs from Piroska and Katalin É. Kiss, the two Budapest-based young literary scholars who helped the author to assemble her memoirs and who edited them for publication.

I confess that I first viewed the manuscript with some suspicion. Having lately read, at the request of various journals, a great many memoirs by Holocaust survivors and other victims of World War II terror and persecution, I had begun to wonder whether less would not have been more in this literary genre.

It may be that Primo Levi, Aleksandr Solzhenitsyn, and similar highly educated, profoundly inspired, and shatteringly honest survivors have told us everything worth knowing about the horrors of World War II and its aftermath. Their epigons often seem to write according to well-established standards, repeating what is well-known, emphasizing their own beneficial role, and, because of advanced age, sometimes unable to distinguish between what they heard, what they read, and what they personally experienced. The reason for writing seems to be their need to unburden themselves of terrible and often suppressed recollections; this is good and understandable psychologically but not always very useful from the point of view of history.

What can one expect, I wondered, from the reminiscences of an old woman living in virtual isolation in Ruthenia, one of Europe's poorest and, until recently, one of its most isolated regions? The many amateur photographs in the manuscript, depicting friends and family members, mostly identified by disconcertingly informal nicknames, did not seem very promising either. Only when reading the piece did I realize how honest, entertaining, and disturbing her story is. What will strike the reader, among other things, is the admirable modesty of the author and her excellent memory. Unlike many other memoirists, she does not focus on herself more than is necessary; nor does she claim to have been a hero, although in many respects she must have been one; nor does she attempt to re-invent minor events and complex dialogues that took place many decades ago. Mary Halász tells what she remembers and not what she would like to remember.

This is a unique oeuvre, not only because it describes life in a region that has been so seldom described for Western audiences, but also because it has been written by an American woman, whom romance had brought to Ruthenia's largest city Uzhhorod (in Hungarian: Ungvár) and its surroundings more than sixty years ago. For all practical purposes, Mary Halász has not left the region since that time. During those sixty odd years she has experienced both great evil and great goodness; she has lived through three changes of state and many more changes in the form of government. Starting out in Czechoslovakia as a young American of seventeen years of age, she saw her region become part of Hungary, then of the Soviet Ukraine, and finally, of Ukraine pure and simple. All this, with brief interludes of Rusyn (Ruthenian) strivings for autonomy or even independence.

Mary Halász was born in 1921 in a region that, until the end of World War I, had been northeastern Hungary; at the time of her birth it was Czechoslovakia. She was a mere infant when her Hungarian-speaking family left for the United States and settled in Roebling, New Jersey, to build a comfortable working-class existence. Their life centered around the Roebling Company, manufacturers of wiring among other things, that employed Mary's father for thirty-five years. It was as a young teenager that she first visited Ruthenia, in far-eastern Czechoslovakia, and it was to this region that she returned late in 1937 to marry Sándor Laszota, a Hungarian teacher with whom she had fallen in love during her first visit. Theirs must have been a charming and elegant wedding, which Mary describes with loving care. Since then, the two have loyally shared their lives, despite long periods of enforced separation.

The first separation occurred when Sándor served in the Czechoslovak army as an officer in the reserves, called upon to defend the country against German and, possibly, Hungarian invasion. He was away when, in the fall of 1938, Mary, with her friends and relatives, celebrated Hungary's take-over of the region. Soon thereafter, Sándor was called up to serve in the war, this time as an officer in the reserves of the Hungarian army. Nineteen-forty-four was their first harrowing year, marked, among other things, by the deportation to Auschwitz, under the aegis of the Hungarian authorities, of her best friend, a young Jewish woman. It continued with the arrival of the Soviet army in Ruthenia, and the customarily brutal Soviet "liberation."

In the following years, the Soviets and local Communists confiscated and nationalized all that could be taken over by the state and, finally, in 1949, they arrested, tried, and sentenced Sándor on trumped-up charges. He spent the next six years in one of the worst camps of the Gulag. Mary describes well how almost the entire non-Slavic intelligentsia of the region—Hungarian teachers, Greek Catholic priests, businessmen, artists, etc.—were sent to Siberia or were made forever to disappear. The Soviets' goal was to rid Ruthenia of its Hungarian, German, remaining Jewish, and even certain Rusyn educated elements in order to create a new elite that was unconditionally loyal to the Soviet Ukrainian state.

Yet the most exciting parts of the book are not only the accurate, informative, and useful descriptions of historic events, but the story of economic and cultural crises brought about by the period's mindless and brutal regimes. Hungarian rule between 1938 and 1944 does not escape some well-deserved criticism, but the chief culprit is, of course, Soviet Bolshevism. How much unnecessary suffering! How harrowing it must have been for Mary to try to obtain permission to travel from Ruthenia to Moscow to claim her United States passport! How humiliating for her to meet her mother after a separation of twenty-five years, not in Uzhhorod where she was living, but in L'viv, the nearest place her American mother was allowed to visit as a tourist. Even in that city the two were forced to stay in separate wings of their hotel, and could meet only under the vigilant eyes of the mother's official guide.

It is a miracle that Mary Halász never really despaired, not even when, after the war, the US Embassy denied a visa to her husband whom they considered an "enemy alien." In fact, Mary has not been back to the United States in over sixty years; nor is it likely that she will ever return.

Although still a citizen of the United States, and of that country alone, Mary and her husband have accepted to live out their lives in Ruthenia, today a bankrupt place plagued by inflation and by shortages of electricity, water, and fuel. Still, Ruthenia is their beloved home.

Throughout the book Mary never fails to mention how well people of different religions (Jews, Roman Catholics, Greek Catholics, Greek

Orthodox) and nationalities (Rusyns, Hungarians, Germans, Slovaks, Romanians, Czechs) once lived together in the region, and how ethnic cleansing that was imposed from abroad during and just after World War II has put an end to that enviable state of affairs. In Ruthenia, as Mary Halász writes at the end of this fascinating book, she has come to understand how many good, strong, and honest people there are in the world. "I owe thanks," she concludes, "to my friends, acquaintances, and unknown persons for giving us lodging when we had no place to go; for sending us milk in the mornings when the children needed it the most; or for forwarding Sanyi's letters to us, thereby keeping alive the hope in all of us. As an American housewife I would certainly have had much less experience with these human qualities."

István Deák
Columbia University
New York, New York

Co-author's Note

We came to know about the exceptional life of Mary Halász from her daughter, Aurelia, who had been our friend and neighbor in Budapest. When, in 1995, we had a chance to get acquainted with Mary Halász in person, and to listen to her own vivid narrative, we asked her to let us record and publish her memoirs. After some hesitation, she agreed. We recorded her words by a tape recorder in several sessions in Budapest during 1996 and 1997. We checked her recollections concerning historical events in various published sources (her statements turned out to be surprisingly accurate), and we supplemented them with a few dates and figures taken from the historical literature. We also interviewed her husband about his Gulag experiences.

The texts of the interviews were arranged into coherent units by Piroska É. Kiss. Although Ms. Halász's native language is English, the interviews were conducted in Hungarian, the language of communication among us. The English text was prepared by Katalin É. Kiss. Whereas Ms. Halász referred to places which had belonged to Hungary until 1919 by their Hungarian names, this text gives their present official versions—in keeping with the policy of the Carpatho-Rusyn Research Center. The first time a place is mentioned, it is followed by the Hungarian equivalent in parentheses.

Piroska and Katalin É. Kiss
Budapest, Hungary
December, 1998

From America with Love

CHAPTER 1

E very Halász, Daddy's whole family, were building contractors in Leles (Hungarian: Lelesz) a Magyar- (Hungarian-) inhabited village in former Zemplén county of present-day Slovakia. That was not such a large-scale business as it is nowadays, but it went well and earned the family a decent living. When a flooding of the Latorytsia (Latorca) swept their house away, they became homeless. However, it was not poverty that drove them to America; they thought emigration would offer them more possibilities. Almost everybody emigrated from the large, closely-knit, warm family of my father.

My father, István Halász, was twenty-eight when he arrived in the New World in 1920. His two brothers and his sister were already there— he was the last to arrive. At the beginning it was not clear if he would find what he was after in America. He went to his eldest brother in New Jersey. First he washed dishes in a hotel, but then he soon found work in his own trade. It helped that by then both of his brothers had good names as masons. It did not take long before he arranged the documents and sent his family the tickets to come over by ship. By that time he had decided he wanted to stay. He never returned to Europe, even though he suffered from homesickness. He could not bear the long voyage. He became so seasick that he had to be carried on shore on a stretcher. He would not have risked crossing the ocean once more.

Most of my mother's family remained in Leles. My mother, Mária Bodnár, was nine when she lost her mother. At that time her father emigrated to America and took his young son with him. There he remarried and had another child. (I still remember when we met my grandfather for the first time in America. From that time on we kept in touch, but seldom saw each other because they lived far away, in Detroit, Michigan.) Mommy stayed in Leles. Her grandmother would not allow her to go to a strange country and decided to raise my mother herself. Mommy remained deeply attached to her grandparents and continued to visit them even after she had become a young American wife. She was loved and accepted in Leles by her many aunts, uncles, cousins, and school-mates. Before she took my sister and me to visit Leles, she had previously gone to see her relatives twice. On those occasions she left us in America with our aunt. She had a Czechoslovak passport, because my parents got American citizenship only when I was eight or nine years old.

Mommy married Daddy at a very young age. She was exactly twenty when she had me, and I was already her second child. She had a son before me who unfortunately died. Daddy left for America alone because she was pregnant with me and close to term. Poor Mommy nearly died when giving birth to me, as I weighed almost fourteen pounds! And I was brought into the world in the natural way, at home, with the helping hands of a midwife! In those days, newborn babies were almost immediately christened. When our priest saw the big baby, he wondered why such a good religious family waited so long before having their child christened. He could not believe I was only five days old!

I was about six months old when the tickets that Daddy sent us arrived, and we set out after him. Mommy also took the eldest daughter of an uncle, Anna, with us, and so it was three of us who got on board in Hamburg. During the fourteen-day voyage to New York I was the passengers' favorite, so that besides feeding me, Mommy did not have much to care about.

By the time we arrived, Daddy had obtained a lovely two-storey four-room house with modern conveniences in a settlement called Roebling, built by the Roebling's Sons Company for its workers ten miles south of Trenton, New Jersey. The houses belonging to the company could be rented very cheaply, and water and electricity were provided free. We were very content living there. Later we moved on to ever larger and more beautiful houses, but I spent all my happy American years in Roebling.

The Roebling Company manufactured all types of wire from cables and wire ropes to tiny wires used in watches, but it was best known for building many of the famous suspension bridges of America, among them the Brooklyn Bridge over the East River. The huge site of the wiremill lay on both banks of the Delaware River, on which the raw materials and the finished products were shipped. Daddy was employed by the Company as a maintainer of the furnaces. He held this position until he retired. Once I received a newspaper clipping with a long article praising Daddy and some of his fellow workers, and also showing their photos commemorating the thirty-five years that they had been working for the Roebling's Sons Company.

Everybody in Roebling worked for the Wire Company, including many women. The Company treated its employees very well, and I lived among content people. They received decent wages, three-week paid holidays, as well as medical care. The retirement fund to which they were paying meant real security for their old age. At school too everybody was well-dressed. The lunches that children took to school also demonstrated the prosperity of their families. In addition to sandwiches, cookies, and fruit, everybody had five or ten cents on them for ice cream or chocolate. The school actually offered lunch in a nice dining room, but we preferred to take our own lunches.

Depending on the time one had spent at the Roebling Company, and the advance one had made, one could move on to larger houses in better locations. Roebling was divided by railroad tracks. First we lived outside the tracks, on Amboy Avenue, near the shopping center. Streets 1 to 8, crossed by Main Street, were across the tracks from us. The school, the church, and a lovely park were situated on the right bank of the river. On the left bank, a little residential quarter of privately owned brick houses was just being erected. Daddy also worked on them, for in addition to his maintenance job, he undertook masonry. His work was highly appreciated everywhere; we were invited to every housewarming party.

Our house was equipped with all the household appliances. We had a refrigerator, a washing machine, a vacuum cleaner. We did every messy job, from washing to drawing a chicken, in the basement, so we kept all the machines there. Our dining habits were a mixture of American and Hungarian traditions. On weekdays Mommy usually prepared a quick dinner from canned or half-prepared ingredients. On Saturdays and Sundays, on the other hand, Daddy required Hungarian cooking: chicken-broth, stuffed cabbage, stuffed chicken, and the like.

In those years, many immigrants arrived in Roebling. Mommy supplemented the family income by renting out the upper floor to newcomers. Later she found a job in a nearby dressmaking factory. She liked her work; she sewed pockets or collars on—I don't remember any more. On weekends we could buy the defective pieces of clothing for almost nothing. Those dresses actually looked perfect; the defects that the supervisor of the factory had found in them after a very careful examination were unnoticeable to the non-expert. On Friday afternoons Mommy would buy clothes, one item more beautiful than the other, by the dozen. We wore most of them once or twice, then washed them, and Mommy sent them to our relatives in Leles. At that time (in 1929-1930) only used clothes could be sent to Czechoslovakia.

Not every family had a car yet, so women grouped together to go to work. They shared a car and also the expenses. We did not have a car, either, since Daddy could not drive because of his agoraphobia. Later, after I had left home, they bought a car, and Mommy learned to drive.

In 1923 a sister of mine was born. Around the time when she was expected the midwife moved in with us, and I was taken to my aunt's. I was happy to have the baby, although her constant crying disturbed me. Mommy told me later that I asked, with my hands on my hips: "How long do I still have to rock this baby?" My sister is two years and four months younger than I am. We could only spend our childhood together and we were different in every respect. Even so, we have always loved each other very much.

We moved from our first house fairly soon into a three-storey semi-detached house, which had a garden as well, where Daddy grew chrysanthemums and azaleas in painted tires scattered on the lawn. When entering the house through the front door, you were in a hall which opened onto a sitting room, then further down a family room, a dining room, and off the dining room, a kitchen. On the second floor, opposite the staircase, was the bathroom. Then the corridor turned and led to my room and to my parents' bedroom. My sister's room and the guestroom were on the third floor.

The guestroom was used regularly. We belonged to a big family in America, but only one of Daddy's brothers, Uncle Gellért lived close to us. His other siblings, Uncle Albert and Aunt Mariska lived in one and the same city in Connecticut. We also kept in touch with an aunt of Daddy's from Cleveland. We corresponded about when they would visit us and when we would visit them. My cousin Anna, who accompanied us on our voyage to America, lived in Browns Mill, a village not far from Roebling, where she and her husband grew black currents. Brown's Mill is in a lovely pine forest and has a lake whose water, though crystal-clear, is black because of the roots of black pines. We spent long holidays there and always had a very good time.

Uncle Gellért bought a farm close to us. He had a wonderful house built on it and lived there raising chickens. His three oldest children, Anna, Helen, and Gilbert (a concert violinist) were already grown-up; Anna could have been our mother for her age. Anna made a very good match. She married a man who was practically a millionaire. She often invited us for summer holidays to their house by the seaside.

Uncle Gellért also had a much younger fourth child, Margó, who was exactly my age. We were very close to each other, as if we were sisters, Margó Halász and I, Mary Halász. We went to the same class from nursery to high school. Mommy and Margó's mom, my aunt, took us to school in turns. Since in many families both parents worked, children stayed in school at least until four o'clock. I still remember our nursery school teacher and the games we used to play. It was such a nice period of my life. In that part of the world, people don't like to go outside when everything is covered by ice. We enjoyed school so much that Mommy, sliding and tumbling, had to pull us to school on a sledge even on such days.

Since we attended an American school, we spoke excellent English. In order to acquire American citizenship, our parents had to pass a difficult exam in the English language and the American Constitution. Since they wanted to learn English, we spoke English at home. In fact, they learned English from us. As a consequence, we children did not learn to speak Hungarian, although we understood it.

I proved to be such a smart little girl that I could start school at the age of five. I loved school. There were all kinds of competitions: who was late, who was not; who was absent, who was not, etc. We enthusiastically collected the scores. I wanted school—and the scores—so much that I was never late. When I felt unwell, I did not tell Mommy. I went to school even with a high fever. It happened that I ended up in the sick-room, but for several years I had not been absent and I had not been late, coming out on top in my class. We had the same teacher in the first four grades. She taught us to read, to count, to write, and to spell. Spelling was my favorite subject. Our teacher taught it in a playful, competitive way, so the children tried very hard. To this day, when I see a new word, I spell it to myself. We also noticed that our nice young lady teacher was always met by a male teacher after school. We gossiped about them with great relish. I loved all the eight years that I spent at our state school. I was even fond of its large, stern building.

We had obligatory religious instruction Friday afternoons in the

Roman Catholic church. On Fridays school ended earlier, but it was strictly checked whether we all showed up in the church afterwards. On Saturdays and Sundays there was no school, but we had our chores at home. We kept our own rooms in order, we changed our bedsheets, etc. The sooner we were done with our chores, the sooner we could go out.

One had to go to Trenton for theater and concerts, but my parents were not interested in them. Roebling had a library where we were regular customers. The cinema in Roebling was closed for some reason, so if we felt like seeing a film, we had to go to Trenton or to Burlington. We often did, because Mommy (just like I) adored movies. At the cinema, there was a non-stop program. Between two shows, acrobats, comedians, and other vaudeville artists entertained the audience. Once you bought a ticket, you could stay for any amount of time, so we often saw a film twice or even three times. Mommy enjoyed movies so much that we usually stayed for two shows for the price of one ticket. Those were charming films; even the simplest ones had something to say to us.

As for Daddy, his family was everything to him, and he knew how to express his love. No matter how tired he came home from work, we could always persuade him to take us to the movies. Poor Daddy would try to suggest "let us wait until tomorrow," but if we could not wait to see the latest Shirley Temple or Janet McDonald film, he gave in and changed into nice clothes. He wore jeans only to work. He had summer, autumn, and winter jeans, in blue and grey colors, but after work he did not wear anything but dark trousers and a white shirt with short sleeves in summer and long sleeves in winter. I never saw him wear anything else.

Mommy was also an exceptionally elegant woman. She loved beautiful clothes. And I do, too. Mommy, naturally, knew how to sew, as in her time girls were taught that. Still she did not use her skill, because she did not need to. She could afford to buy what she wanted. I was more interested in knitting and crocheting, and these skills were fashionable among the girls. I learned knitting from a friend of mine, Betty, when I was about nine or ten years old. I made wonderful pieces for myself. Embroidery, on the other hand, was not in fashion. I learned it first here in Europe at a much older age.

On weekends in the summer our parents took us to the beach, as it was only at an hour's distance from our place. These excursions were European style. We went together with our friends, and we took picnic baskets along with chicken fried in breadcrumbs and delicious homemade cookies. On our way there we stopped to have a snack in a lovely pine forest where we could already hear the roaring of the ocean. The boardwalk and the pier at Seaside Heights were like a fantastic amusement park. There were all kinds of entertainment: games, a shooting range, slot machines, a music pavilion. My cousin and I sometimes also went to Atlantic City, which was even richer and more entertaining.

We had a beautiful, quiet childhood. We had great toys, played marbles, and skipped rope, but I loved my dolls the best. I got wonderful dolls as presents. The largest one I used to push about in a carriage. It was even more fun to turn a shoebox into a pram for a smaller doll. I sewed a little pillow and a little cover to fit it, and I pulled it with a rope after me. The main scene of my playing with dolls was the stairlanding, where my dolls lived in an armchair. My mother told me—when we met in Hungary in 1971—that she had kept my most beautiful doll and always washed her dress before Christmas.

We were playful kids and nobody disturbed us in our games. In summer after it rained we were allowed to wade in the pools of water left on the sidewalk. We got together with a large, mixed group of children from our street every day. In our immediate neighborhood alone there lived Serbian, Czech, Hungarian, Lithuanian, and Black American kids. We were on very good terms with them, even if we were intimate only with the children of our own little circle. All the kids from our street, as well as our classmates, were invited to our birthday parties, and, naturally, we were also invited to their parties.

The Hungarians stuck together in Roebling and even founded an association in which Daddy had some function. They organized Anna balls, Stephen's Day parties, and vintage balls in the assembly hall. We children also took part in these entertainments, and nobody was left out. At night the caretaker of the assembly hall put the children to sleep somehow so that parents could stay longer. They knew how to pass the time well. They sought out good music on the radio, listened to good records, and of course they sang a lot. My parents also had beautiful voices and loved singing. It is an amusing memory of mine that as a child I heard and memorized *a lábamon alig-alig állok, mégis szeretnek a lányok*, and kept singing *alabali galigaligali, megi gali galigali* for years with a deep conviction. I laughed when years later the sense of the text ("I barely stand on my feet, still girls love me") became clear to me.

According to American custom, name days were not celebrated, except for Stephen's Day, but it fell on Christmas Day, anyway. We celebrated Christmas and Easter beautifully; always together, one day at our place, the other day at the Ronyeczes', Orbans', or my godparents' place. Our Christmas menu, on the other hand, was already American style, with turkey and apple pie. The Christmas tree was also decorated in the American way; instead of candy in Christmas wrappings, we hung strings of little electric lights and lovely garlands on the tree.

The Hungarians as good, conscientious American citizens also celebrated the great American holidays: Thanksgiving and Labor Day. We children spoke in English on these holidays, even when in Hungarian company. The adults talked to us in English, but they spoke with each other in Hungarian.

CHAPTER 2

I t was after the seventh grade in the summer that Mommy first took us kids, with her to Europe. I was the smallest child in our class, a sickly, anemic little girl, so the doctor ordered me a change of air. We could have gone to California or Florida, but Mommy was longing for her former homeland. Therefore my parents decided that the change of air should be Europe: "The children must know where they come from!" They also wanted to have the opinion of a doctor from "back home" on how I could become healthier.

We set out for Europe on board a ship called Bremen in New York. The sea was rough, tossing the ship about, only for half a day. Otherwise the weather was excellent. Mommy soon made friends with our fellow passengers; she enjoyed herself. We had a nice three-bed cabin with a round porthole in tourist class. Dining took place in turns, in very elegant surroundings. The children on board were looked after by qualified teachers in a playroom all day long. This way both the adults could spend the seven days of the voyage completely carefree, and the large, mixed group of children assembled on board had a lot of fun. I still remember two Greek girls who also went visiting their parents' native country together with their mother. Well, they put on their national costume already a day before landing. That was how they greeted Europe. Or perhaps it had been arranged that they would wear it so that they could be recognized by the people meeting them.

We landed in Bremen. We were not expected; Mommy wanted our visit to be a surprise. We took a train to Prague, then another one to Král'ovský Chlmec (Hungarian: Királyhelmec), where, on our arrival at night, Mommy found a horse-carriage to take us to Leles, which had no railway. We went to one of Daddy's three cousins' still in Leles, Uncle András. Mommy's grandmother was not alive any more, but she had lots of other relatives there. We only stayed until Mommy decided whether we should go on to Mukachevo (Munkács) or Uzhhorod (Ungvár). Eventually she decided on Uzhhorod, where she found— through an advertisement—a one-room apartment. The local doctor said that a one-month change of air was not worth anything. My parents discussed this through correspondence, and, as a result, we stayed for eight months. Daddy sent us money every month.

Mommy enrolled us in a convent school called Gizella-ház. A South American girl and the two of us were the only foreign students of the school. Children were taught in combined grades by nuns. The first four grades, the fifth and sixth grades, and the seventh and eighth grades studied together. Although I had finished the seventh grade in America, I entered into the fifth grade of the Hungarian school. I learned Hungarian very fast—unlike my sister who was not interested in the Hungarian language at all. Perhaps it was a sense of what would come that made me learn Hungarian. I must have felt I would need it some day. We had to recite lessons just like the others, and we often made our class laugh. It was especially my sister who talked nonsense. Even our extremely serious priest, who taught us religion, could barely resist laughing when we answered his questions in Hungarian. Nevertheless, we received our certificates in the end. It made me very happy that I received good marks.

In Uzhhorod we soon established our own little social circle, al- though when we had arrived, we knew no one except Aunt Olga, a distant relative. Mommy was familiar with the city only to the extent that once she had been there on a mineral water cure together with a friend of hers from Leles. Mommy knew how to make friends, and she lived an interesting, colorful life in Uzhhorod, as well. She would often go, together with Aunt Olga, the Kleins, and others, to hear Gypsy music, or to have a wine and picnic party on the row of wine cellars.

On such occasions the children, Aunt Olga's daughter, Editke Klein, and we two, gathered in one of our houses, where we played together, had supper, and went to bed. Once we went to the movies in the after- noon. We saw King Kong, and then the four of us were left alone! I will never forget the terror we felt. We wanted no supper, nothing. We only prayed cuddled up together that Mommy would come home soon!

In Uzhhorod, there was a women's club which held tea parties in the garden of Hotel Korona. At one of these tea parties a special beauty pageant was organized for little girls. The women's club issued tickets for the benefit of the poor, and the girl who could sell the most tickets became the winner. Well, at the age of thirteen I became the beauty queen and won the first prize: a doll. It was a brown-haired sleeping-doll, which was to be the most beautiful of all my dolls. It is the doll that my mother, now ninety six, still has, and keeps dressing up.

We would often go for walks. Uzhhorod has a wonderful section called Galago, with a lovely walkway along the bank of the river Uzh (Ung), that begins from the promenade at the foot bridge. The promenade was also very spectacular. A point of it was called the "Awkward corner." It was at that corner that young men gathered and waited, and then dispersed one by one to join their sweethearts appearing on the promenade. The promenade was crowded and bustling on weekend afternoons, too, but the real parade took place on Sunday mornings after church, in a festival mood. There was a music pavilion with promenade concerts and other amusements that belong to a proper promenade. Ladies showed off their new dresses and hats, arm in arm with their husbands. On Sunday mornings the citizens of Uzhhorod—craftsmen, merchants, civil servants, professionals, Roman Catholics, Greek Catholics, Jews, Hungarians, Czechs, and other nationalities—all passed the time together with their families in the inner city, in mutual tolerance and understanding.

Uzhhorod citizens made a living from their trade or business. On Thursdays, fairs were held. Craftsmen worked for the whole week so that they could have enough products to sell at the fair. My future father-in-law—a trueborn Uzhhorod craftsman, a harness maker with an assistant—was also there every Thursday.

We rented our apartment from the Moncsák family, who were teachers, and who had such a big house that they rented out two apartments in it. We always played quietly so that we would not disturb the landlady. She was ill, and nevertheless she was glad that we brought a little cheerfulness into the house. Her children were already university students in Prague. Irén was to be a teacher, and Béla studied medicine. They also liked us. Béla was learning English and tried to practice the language with us. Eventually we became close friends. After we returned home my sister corresponded with Béla, and by the time she became an adult a sincere affection had evolved between them. Béla would have gladly visited her in America, but then it was already impossible. All of his applications were turned down.

It only turned out much later that I also found my sweetheart owing to the Moncsák house in Uzhhorod. I was still a little girl, and he was already a teacher, whom I greeted as children greet adults, with "I kiss your hand, Uncle Sanyi!" Uncle Sanyi had a diploma from the teachers training college in Mukachevo, after an interlude at the law school in Bratislava (Hungarian: Pozsony). His sister, Ilonka, my future sister-in-law, lived with her husband, a merchant, in a cute little apartment opening onto our courtyard. She became a good friend of mine. I got to know Sanyi, then a handsome, well-built, twenty-two or twenty-three year-old young man, when he was visiting his sister. Sanyi was already courting a girl who appeared to encourage his advances. At that time I did not feel any love for him yet, but we became friends. I still remember one of our first encounters in the courtyard. "What are you doing, Mary?" he asked. "A button has gotten torn off my shoe; I am trying to fix it." He took it from me and sewed it up with his strong hands. I thanked him politely. He admired how my sister and I could enjoy ourselves, how well we could play together, how enthusiastically we threw the ball about and at the same time never stopped talking.

My sister and I had our confirmation ceremony in Uzhhorod; even the bishop was present at it. Aunt Olga became my sister's godmother, and my future sister-in-law became mine. So we parted as relatives when the time came for us to return home. Apparently I had grown and had become chubbier, and Daddy was longing to see us very much. So he sent us the tickets for our passage.

My relationship with Mr. Sanyi started when we said good-bye to each other. It was then that we agreed that we would correspond with each other. My dear Mr. Sanyi made me promise that I would write to him on arriving home, which I did. He answered my little letter, and I also answered his, as was proper to do. And we have come so far! When parting, I received from him a wonderful photo, which he dedicated to me. In Roebling, I bragged about it to the other girls of my age, who said: "It is easy to show off with the photo of a Hungarian actor!" My Mr. Sanyi looked like a film star!

Mommy loved travelling, and therefore she always picked a different route. This time we left for Genoa, Italy, via Yugoslavia, after an unforgettable visit to Venice. Because of some terrorist actions, the Yugoslavian border guard looked everywhere for explosives. He even wanted to cut open the stomach of my doll! I sobbed my heart out. I asked the border guard if he had a daughter. He did have one! "What would your daughter say if the stomach of her favorite doll were cut open?" I asked. I told him how I had won the doll at a beauty pageant and where I was travelling with it. He took pity on me eventually. Mommy told me she had never experienced such a strict customs examination.

Before leaving, naturally, we paid a farewell visit to all of our friends. We took a cab to the Uzhhorod railway station, then a train to Budapest, where we had to find our travel agency. There, in the office, a family was saying good-bye in tears to their only daughter. Mommy noticed that they mentioned Jersey and Trenton, and, as was typical of her, she got acquainted with the people right away. Well, Gizike, their daughter, was going to America to get married there. She had never been to America before, she had never met her fiancé, and she could not speak a word of English. Mommy took her under her wing, to Gizike's and her family's great relief. We travelled together and kept up the relationship later as well. In fact, the rest of my family and Gizike have been friends to this day. Mommy even became the godmother of one of Gizike's children. Gizike's parents-in-law were looking for a Hungarian wife for their son, John. John got to know Gizike, who was nearly thirty then, through correspondence. He was a third-generation emigrant and could not speak a word of Hungarian. Despite all this, the marriage turned out to be perfect. John brought Gizike to our house once every fortnight for a whole evening so that she could have a good chat in Hungarian.

Daddy was informed by the travel agency which day and on which ship we would arrive. My dear father could not wait to get his family back at last!

In Genoa we got on board a large, beautiful Italian passenger steamship called Compe di Savoya. As before, we had a three-bed cabin with a porthole in tourist class. We insisted on having a porthole, although this time we did not make much use of it. This is because Gizike spent practically the whole day with us and returned to her own cabin only to sleep. It was hard to get used to the constant hubbub of those noisy Italians. It was also difficult for us to get used to Italian food, with the obligatory tomato sauce and cheese! They put cheese on everything, even the soup!

The first day of our journey was lovely, and so was the second. We stopped at some island belonging to Africa, and we bought fruit from the natives. They sold many different kinds of fruit, some of which I had never seen before or after, in woven baskets made of sedge. It was there that I ate fresh figs for the first time in my life. They did not resemble their well-known dried, pressed, sweet variety at all. The grapes were unbelievably large! The natives also sold fruits I knew: pineapples, bananas, and the like.

Then, on the third day, an awful storm overtook us, which raged for three days. I will never forget that horror! The sea, which is so beautiful in normal circumstances, can turn into hell! It tossed us frontwards, backwards, sidewards—from every direction. The engines stopped working. We were at the mercy of the raging wind, which threw us about. There was no knowing where we were. The ship sent out SOS signals but could not give its coordinates.

The portholes of the cabins were closed by iron covers, and so we could not look out any longer. It was frightening that no matter how tightly the porthole was shut, some water seeped through from time to time. The chairs were fastened to hooks in the floor. Meals were accompanied by unbelievable scenes. It happened that the bowl of soup just brought in by the waiter landed on the lap of a young woman sitting next to me. There was incessant shrieking, crying, and shouting.

Mommy decided that if people were ordered to flee to the lifeboats we would not leave because the hysterical crowd would certainly stampede us. Mommy, Gizike, my sister, and I sat on the bed and prayed. Mommy kept saying: "God will help us!"

I proved to be a curious child even under these circumstances. The first day—not realizing the danger we were in—I was still strolling about, holding on to things. There was also a playroom on this ship. I felt too big to play, but I would go there to chat and make friends. Sailors were coming and going, fixing the equipment on the deck. Imitating them, I opened the little hatchway through which we would normally go out for a walk. The wind immediately got hold of me and started to suck me out with unbelievable force. Fortunately, a sailor noticed what was happening, pulled me back with great difficulty, and slammed the door. He asked aghast what I was doing. "I wanted to see how the wind was blowing, " I said. I also admitted to Mommy that I was almost blown away by the wind when I wanted to look out. I got away without a spanking, but I was still trembling for quite a while afterwards.

The following day the captain himself came down to the tourist class to calm the people, telling them that everything was all right. In fact, not everything was, as the ship had a small leak in it. The news about the leak soon got out, and the hysterical crowd became even more excited.

The third day of the storm was already too much for the passengers to bear. Almost everybody was sick and many were vomiting. Hardly anyone showed up in the dining room. I had no problem with eating— I felt perfectly fine. Mommy also ate well. Gizike did so less, and she often felt sick. Dining was made possible by frames built on the tables. Most of the furniture was also fastened to the ground. The ship almost completely heeled from time to time and we thought it was going to sink.

And what a wonder: in the evening of the third day, the storm abruptly vanished without leaving a trace. Either we got out of it, or it was sucked up into the sky. I don't know. The loudspeaker announced that it was over and everyone could relax. Then it turned out that the ship had drifted off its course. My father learned all this from the radio. It was on the fourth day of the six-day voyage that hell broke loose, and we arrived in New York only on the ninth day! I can imagine what Daddy went through.

We were very happy to touch land in the end. We went through the customs examination and then arranged for our luggage to be put on a porter's cart. We accumulated lots of luggage during our long stay. Mommy liked European girls' dresses, and so she had sailor suits, checkered suits with plaited skirts, blouses decorated with embroidery and drawn work, etc., made for us. This kind of needlework was unknown in America, so our blouses were very much admired. We also received dirndls with little aprons as present. After arriving home, Mommy took many pictures of us wearing our dazzling new outfits.

Mommy got us ashore, to the railway station, and into the train without any help. She did all this with innumerable pieces of luggage (in fact, huge trunks), with two kids, and apparently with no problem. I only started wondering as a grown-up how she had ever managed! Gizike also had plenty of luggage; she had brought along her whole trousseau. She was met by her new family including her fiancé, whom she had not seen before, in New York. As agreed through correspondence in advance, they wore white berets, and in addition to that, John held an American flag, and Gizike held a Hungarian one.

Actually, I never liked New York. I had been there more than once before, but I did not have pleasant experiences in the city, perhaps because of my aversion to masses of people. We set out from Grand Central Station on 42nd Street. Daddy was waiting for us in Trenton. He could not tolerate staying in New York until we arrived. He kept inquiring about the expected time of our arrival, and when we called at

18

the harbor, he hurried to Trenton to meet us there. In Trenton we took another train, this time together with Daddy. We were heading home at last!

CHAPTER 3

I n Trenton, a delicious dinner prepared by Mommy's friends awaited us. What a great surprise! When we had left for Europe, Daddy moved over to a family whom we knew well, and while we were away, he rented, renovated, and furnished a much nicer house in a much better location than the one we had lived in before. So we arrived in a new house, on 5th Street in the center of Roebling near the park. It resembled our previous house, but it had a nicer kitchen, a bigger living room, and a much more elegant hall and staircase.

We did not have a parquet floor, but Daddy learned a very interesting, beautiful way of painting the wooden floor. First he applied a certain shade of brown, than a shade of beige, then a different shade of brown again. When the third layer was also about to dry, Daddy dragged a little engraved roller over it, which produced a moire effect. I still remember him doing this.

For Mommy's birthday, Daddy bought new furniture for the living room, he had new curtains made, had the stairs covered with a new carpet, and had the bedroom refurnished. It looked to me then like the dream bedrooms we had seen in films. In the living room we had a sofa, Daddy's armchair with a high back, and smaller armchairs with a Gobelin pattern which my parents were especially fond of. We also had a piano with a player piano mechanism built into it. If we put a perforated record into the player piano and pressed a pedal, the keys started to move by themselves and played Hungarian songs, to Daddy's greatest delight. Even if reluctantly, I also played the piano myself. My sister, on the other hand, could not be persuaded to learn to play it, so the piano had an unfortunate fate after my departure.

Our household went through a marvellous transformation. The gas cooker ignited by itself, without the use of matches. We had a standing vacuum cleaner, the type which is coming into fashion here in Ukraine only now. Naturally, we had a refrigerator, too. We washed up in a porcelain double sink with a dish drainer. The varnished floor only needed mopping. We used a mop in the middle of which there was a little sponge to attract dust. It made cleaning very simple, and it only needed to be rinsed after cleaning.

All the houses were of a similar arrangement, so our new house, too, had a little garden with a lawn and flowers. We had no vegetable plot because we did not need it. The greengrocer came twice a week. He stopped at every fifth house, and those who needed vegetables or fruit could buy them from his cart. The baker also delivered bread to every house. He put the things we had ordered outside the front door. The milkman and the newspaperman did so, too. They collected the money and the new orders on Saturdays.

We went to the grocer's to buy our lunches, on the other hand, because we picked something different every day: two slices of ham, or salami, etc. Each of us also got his or her favorite cookie. Mommy also baked European cakes: cream rolls, cream buns, fruit flan, but usually only on holidays. She never made leavened cakes so typical of Hungarian cuisine, because, she said, the ones we could buy were so delicious that it was not worth taking trouble with baking them at home. We did our weekly shopping in such a way that on Friday one of us took the shopping list to the grocer's, and on Saturday we got everything delivered. In Roebling, you would not see housewives carrying heavy shopping loads. The minor daily shopping was the chore of us girls.

We went shopping on rollerskates. The store was on the other side of the railway, and before crossing the tracks it was obligatory to take the skates off. At the station, however, my uncle Gellért (the one with the farm) was the track watchman, and he turned a blind eye if I crossed the tracks with my skates on. I had never had any trouble crossing the tracks with my skates until once the last wheel of one of my skates got stuck in the track on which a train was approaching! My uncle looked at the scene paralyzed. Fortunately, the railwayman who was on guard on the other side signalled to the driver of the train in time, and the train was able to stop right in front of me.

After that I was called "the skating queen" by my family. They did not spank me though. They never did. It was enough if Daddy lowered the newspaper and looked at me over it. Mommy, on the other hand, made us kneel if we had done something wrong until we apologized. If I made a mistake, I went up to her right away and promised her that it would never happen again. My sister, on the other hand, would never do that! No matter how much I would urge her she would keep repeating she had not done anything wrong. On such occasions it was she who felt offended! And she was hard to appease.

Since we arrived home in the middle of the summer, we still had a long vacation to enjoy till the beginning of the school year. Daddy even took us to a summer resort. Because of our adventure in Uzhhorod I lost a year at school, but I did not mind. The experiences that I gained during that trip were worth it! My friends went on to the next grade, but my dear Margó stayed with me—she had failed! Before I left for Europe, we had always done our homework together. In fact, we had done everything together. Without me she proved to be slow, even lazy. It was she who missed me the most, and she had simply waited for me.

And then came the eighth grade, which we completed quietly, in good spirits. We had a nice graduation ceremony. Our dear music teacher had been dutifully coaching the choir of the school for it. I was an enthusiastic member of the choir, but I had an awful voice, so she asked me discretely to sing in a quiet voice. I still have two class photos and a "Diploma for the American Penman," but everything else, my yearbooks and other diplomas, got lost during the war. I regret their disappearance very much because I am very attached to such mementos.

After the eighth grade I entered a high school which offered different kinds of specialized training. All of us had to study English, history, and geography, but mathematics, physics, chemistry, and biology were obligatory only for those who wanted to study medicine, engineering, or the like, afterwards. One could also specialize in law or languages. My friends were scattered in the different types of classes. For example, one of them chose languages, which meant that she studied Latin, German, and French, besides English. Our school did not offer a diploma, but the specialized training it provided prepared its students both for various kinds of jobs and for university studies.

The specialization I chose was called "commerce." In fact, we received special training in economics. In addition to the general subjects, we learned bookkeeping, typewriting, and shorthand. Every school day began with reading from the Bible and reciting the Lord's Prayer, which was followed by a five- to ten-minute "admonition" by our formmaster. There were about thirty students in our class, half of them boys, half of them girls, of mixed color and nationalities. We got along with each other very well. Boys and girls had every class together, even sports. In the schoolyard, on the other hand, we played separately.

We also learned to dance at school. School dances were organized on holidays such as Halloween, Thanksgiving, and New Year's Eve. Theater performances were also regularly held. Dramatized versions of famous novels were performed. Since I was a shy little girl, I did not take part in these, but I enjoyed them very much as a spectator.

The first-year students of our high school went to Florence. We were taken there by a school bus. It always arrived according to schedule, and everybody had his or her seat on it, just like in the classroom. There was an early bus and a late bus every morning and every afternoon, because not everybody had the same timetable at school. For example, if we wanted to become better in shorthand, we had to take extra lessons and had to stay longer. On such days, we could go home from school only on the second bus. From the second year on, we went to school in Bordentown, which was somewhat farther away. It was a 35- to 40-minute ride. We could actually use that time to complete our homework on the bus. We wanted to have our evenings for roller-skating! That was more important for us than homework, for it was our social life.

I loved my American Indian form-master very much. He and his wife had no children, and they often picked Margó and me up and took us to their home to roast marshmellows. My form-master and his wife had typical Indian features. Their home, their dishes, carpets, and everything else as well, were of the traditional Indian style.

Our class established a Globetrotter Club. We agreed on where we would travel in the summer, and we calculated the membership fee everyone had to pay each week so that we could realize our goal. Our first adventure was a five-day trip to New York. I still remember the view from the top of the Empire State Building and the huge museums of Central Park: the Museum of Natural Science and the Metropolitan Museum. In the following year we went to Niagara Falls for three days. Not only was the sight an unforgettable experience, but also the walk under it in watertight clothes. And that roaring! In 1935, during the presidency of Theodore Roosevelt, we visited Washington, D.C. We looked at all the important government buildings and memorial places. We organized the trip so that it should coincide with the time of cherry-blossoming. The whole city was in blossom. It was like heaven! White houses among white trees on the green lawns.

I also became a member of the YWCA. It had a huge facility in

Trenton, with a swimming pool, tennis courts, a skating ring, and so on. We went there at least once a week—once for a club meeting, then to swim, to roller-skate, or play tennis, as had been planned in advance. On the days of club meetings we were taught etiquette. We could also invite a partner to the skating ring, since we skated in pairs to music. I was very good at skating and I could do all the figures.

My correspondence with Sanyi became more and more regular, although it was quite burdensome for me to write in Hungarian. What I wrote with great effort was corrected by Mommy. First I only wrote about school and school excursions, and he wrote me about the army, the everyday life of an officers training corps. Sanyi had become an officer in the Czechoslovak army in the meanwhile.

Sanyi liked how beautiful, earnest, and innocent a girl I was. He said that I behaved more seriously than the girls in Uzhhorod. He began making hints that he did not look upon me as a little girl any more. He even took my photo with him to the military barracks. As time passed, he wrote more and more beautiful, amorous letters. Our relationship assumed a serious tone through correspondence. I don't know how it turned into love, but it crept into my thoughts. It was Mommy who noticed that I would hurry to the post office in the afternoon to find out whether there was a letter for me.

Sanyi was encouraged by his sister to propose to me before an American boy snatched me away from under his nose. In fact, he had nothing to be afraid of. I had no boyfriend with whom I would go out. There was a boy with whom I used to study together ever since we were little kids. He was two years ahead of me at school. I found out only later that he was seriously interested in me, although we often met. He lived very close to us. He attended the fine arts high school in Trenton. We often took the same train or tram when I went to my club, or came home from it. He never let me know that he paid more attention to me than is usual between neighbors. He made a move only when he learned of my engagement. He came to our house on my last evening at home, thinking perhaps that it was still not too late for him to try to keep me back. He said he had not proposed before because he first wanted to have a solid financial background. He also had a huge bunch of roses sent to my cabin when I boarded the ship to Europe, with a note saying "It is still not too late!"

So I had not been snatched away from Sanyi. After some time he also started to correspond with my parents, and asked for my hand in marriage in writing. Daddy had never even met him, but Sanyi could write such wonderful letters that he convinced Daddy of his excellence. My parents asked me if I wanted him, and respected my decision, although Daddy was quite upset about the prospect of losing me. Our engagement was organized by Sanyi's sister. My Sanyi's engagement ring was brought to me by a woman called Haluska, who lived on the same street in Uzhhorod as Sanyi's family. I got it in August, 1936, and Sanyi got his ring the very same day, in the military barracks. My ring had "Sanyi" engraved in it, and his ring had "Mary."

It was planned that we would get married as soon as I was eighteen. Sanyi asked me to come to Uzhhorod as early as possible so that by the time he was discharged from the army I could learn European customs. I must have been in love to agree to all that—merely on the basis of correspondence! (I had kept all his letters and had taken them with me to Europe, but they got lost in the war together with so many other personal belongings of mine.)

So it happened that after the third year of high school, at the age of seventeen, I left for Europe by myself to get married. Unfortunately, this also meant that I could not finish my thesis. Our high school prepared its students for their trade very thoroughly. My task was to perform the administration and bookkeeping of a large factory for a whole year, concluded by a final balance. I received in a large case all the bills, receipts, accounts, and remittances coming into the factory on every single day of the year. We were able to do a whole year's administration and accounting by ourselves. We were trained through practice to become real experts. I left before finishing my thesis in the hope that I could graduate in Uzhhorod. Mommy and Daddy supported this idea. They thought it would be expedient for me to complete my studies at a European business school once I had chosen to live there. Unfortunately, my family in Uzhhorod thought otherwise!

My sister did not long to return to Uzhhorod. I, on the other hand, enjoyed life in Uzhhorod very much. My future sister-in-law, a childless woman, doted on me, and she let me have the best of everything. Furthermore, I often heard my parents discuss that they would move back to their homeland when they retired. I could not imagine life without my parents! At that time, it still seemed so simple both for Sanyi and me to visit my parents in America and for them to come to us in Europe that I did not think that my decision would mean a final separation from them.

Things have turned out very differently! Looking back, I would have attempted to talk my child out of such an idea. My parents never said "No" to me. They thought: "It is your choice. If you want it, so let it be!" They undertook all the risks, pains, and difficulties of emigration because they wanted their children to lead easier lives in a better world. And I chose to go back from where they had left! It is true that when I made my decision Uzhhorod was not so hopelessly far from America. After all, it belonged to Czechoslovakia, a democratic country where one could live a pleasant middle class life also as a Hungarian. I guess I must have been driven by my love of adventure!

I set off firmly resolved to get married, but Daddy assured me when letting me go that I could always change my mind, and my room would remain mine. I was actually hoping that I could lure my Sanyi to America, but he did not want to leave his homeland. He paid for it dearly later! By the time he was ready to leave, it had become impossible to do so.

CHAPTER 4

D addy bought my ticket for the passage, and we started packing. I received many beautiful things from my parents: linen, bedclothes, wonderful silver cutlery, etc. I also packed my personal belongings, including a diary locked with a key, which I had started as a very little girl. I did not have many books to take along, because I used to read in the Roebling library (which also served as a scene for our social life). I did not pack my roller skates, since I knew that they were unfit for the cobblestones of Uzhhorod. Perhaps I also felt that over there being engaged and rollerskating were incompatible notions. The things that I left at home were put in a box, where they have been waiting for my return ever since. Everything that I was going to take with me was put— mainly by my parents—into a large trunk.

My sister said good-bye to me on the eve of my departure, and she did not want to see me after that. We were very close to each other, and she would have been unable to watch me leave. It was very hard for us to part that evening. We met again as old women, in Budapest in 1981. Then she told me that when at the age of fourteen or fifteen she was left without a sister, she felt as if her arms and legs had been cut off. We had opposite characters: she was lively and outgoing, and I was with-drawn and reserved. Still we loved each other very much and we still do from afar, even if we have seen each other only once since then! Daddy saw me off in Trenton. Although I was hoping we would be together many more times, the good-bye at Trenton was heartbreaking. The last kiss, the last caress, the last hug. Daddy jumped off the train only when it had begun to move. If I had suspected that we might never meet again, I certainly would not have left. None of us thought that there would be a war, and none of us would have ever dreamed that it would bring about such a catastrophic division of the world. Mommy accompanied me to New York. In those days the escorts of passengers could spend the last hour before departure on board, so Mommy came with me to my cabin. It was very painful for both of us to take leave. She nearly pulled me off the ship at the last minute. I had a ticket in tourist class of a liner called the Queen Mary. I shared a double cabin with someone, but she was barely noticeable. She took to her bed at the departure of the ship, and got out of it only when we touched land. Even her medicine was taken to her bed. She was not the only one who did not enjoy the voyage. I, on the other hand, felt splendid. Our last horrible sea adventure did not frighten me. I knew that it would not necessarily happen again. In fact, I enjoyed the voyage beyond description. I regretted very much when it was over.

On these ships great pains were taken to cater to the passengers. Every class had a steward, whose responsibilities included dealing with the travel documents, tending to the sick, and caring for the well-being of passengers in every respect. The steward of the tourist class was an old friend of Daddy's. He had promised Daddy that he would look after me, and he took me up to first class. I could use the swimming pool, and after dinner I could participate in the evening parties. I managed to pull out of my trunk my wonderful, floor-length, tight-fitting, low-cut aquamarine satin evening dress, and the tulle bolero belonging to it, decorated with lots of little buttons, a wonderful collar, and a tiny bouquet of silk flowers. I looked good in it, with my wavy (even if not too plentiful) brown hair. Most people even found me beautiful. I had success in my lovely new dress made for the Uzhhorod balls also at the evening parties in first class. An excellent light music orchestra played tangos and foxtrots, handsome young men entertained the ladies, and I was asked to dance a lot. I went back to tourist class only to sleep and to dine. Fashionable society accepted me.

Our ship stopped in London, and some of the passangers got off there. Its final destination was Cherbourg, from where we were taken on to Paris. Our luggage was also taken care of. I did not even have to touch my trunk before we arrived in Paris. It was a very convenient and elegant way of travelling. I had to wait three days for the next international train, but the price of the ticket for passage included a three-day stay at a nice Paris hotel. I had an opportunity—never to be repeated— to get to know Paris, but I did not take advantage of it! My first impressions of the city were not very appealing, but first and foremost I was eager to arrive at my destination. So I embarked upon a new adventure. In the hotel I got acquainted with a girl from our ship. We found out that both of us were heading for Czechoslovakia, only that she would have to get off the train somewhat earlier. "What are we doing here?" we asked ourselves, and went to the railway station immediately. We managed to pick a slow train which took two and half days to get to Prague! The international express, which left two days later, caught up with us. From Paris to Prague we received meals for our tickets. From Prague to Chop (Csap), however, I did not eat a bite. At a station I heard a vendor calling "Ice cream! Ice cream!" and I bought some, but after American ice cream, I found it so appalling that I could not eat it.

The two of us travelled together until she got off at her town. At the Košice (Kassa) railway station I heard my name called: "I am looking for you, Mary Halász! I am looking for you, Mary Halász!" I got slightly frightened, not knowing what it was all about. I put my head out of the window, saying I was Mary Halász. Well, my sister-in-law sent me a message through a railway official saying that I should get off at Chop, instead of going to Uzhhorod. And so I did. In Chop my sister-in-law and her husband were waiting for me with a cab. We were driven from Chop to their home. I left for my new life on May 27, 1938, and arrived in the first days of June. I was in Uzhhorod to celebrate my seventeenth birthday.

CHAPTER 5

L et me begin with a classic anecdote. An old man, recalling his life, says: "I was born in the Austro-Hungarian Monarchy, I was a toddler in Hungary, I went to school in Czechoslovakia, I got married in Hungary. Then I worked for decades in the Soviet Union, and now I am a pensioner in Ukraine." "Wow, you certainly have moved around an awful lot!" "Actually, I never left Uzhhorod!"

I arrived in Uzhhorod full of happy expectations, not at all suspecting what was ahead of me. If I had known more about the history of the region, if I had known that after World War I it had been a subject of dispute among Czechoslovakia, Hungary, Romania, and Ukraine, perhaps I would have been more wary. But as long as I was not directly threatened, I was not interested in history and politics. Later, on the other hand, it was not possible any more to find out the truth about what was happening to us and why; we were inundated by lies. We have been able to read the facts about the history of this region only in the past few years, in the nineties.

Uzhhorod is the largest city of the region referred to as Subcarpathia, or Ruthenia, which had been an integral part of Hungary for a thousand years, forming its northeastern counties. The region came to be looked upon as a self-contained entity at the end of World War I, after the disintegration of the Austro-Hungarian Monarchy, when the Romanian, the Czechoslovak, and the West Ukrainian states, then in the process of formation, all laid claim to it. The region was a multiethnic territory, where the Slavic Rusyns constituted the largest ethnic group. The Rusyn intelligentsia declared its wish to remain in the Hungarian state as an autonomous unit. Hungary accepted their demands, and in 1918 it declared the territory inhabited by Rusyns an autonomous province, with a Rusyn self-government for administration, education, and religion.

In early 1919, the Czechoslovak, West Ukrainian, and Romanian

29

armies launched simultaneous attacks on the area from different directions, and occupied it. The fate of the territory was eventually decided by the peace treaty of Versailles, and it became part of Czechoslovakia. The peace treaty ordained autonomy with complete self-government for Subcarpathia, which the Czechoslovak government failed to realize.

After Germany and Italy forced the Czechoslovak government to sign the Munich Pact in late September 1938, within a few days the Rusyns finally received their autonomous government. In early November, however, the southern part of their new autonomous province, including its capital Uzhhorod (once again called Ungvár) was awarded to Hungary. What was left of Ruthenia continued to function for a few more months until March 1939, when the province was taken by the Hungarian Army and renamed Subcarpathia (Kárpátalja).

Things did not change until the fall of 1944, when the Soviet Army occupied the region. Although previously, according to a wartime agreement, the Soviets had stated that Czechoslovakia was to be restored with the borders it had before 1938, this did not happen in the case of Subcarpathia. To justify annexation, the local Communist party was restored, and—under the protection of the Soviet Army—it declared that Subcarpathia must join the Soviet Ukraine. On November 26, 1944, representatives of the population were ordered to appear in the city of Mukachevo to declare unification. Ruthenia was officially renamed the Transcarpathian Ukraine, and it became a republic of the Soviet Union with its own government, ministries, etc. We were not aware of all these events. The only thing thing we saw was Russian military occupation. A year later Ruthenia became part of the Ukrainian Soviet Socialist Republic of the Soviet Union. The region and our city also lost their names. It was then that Ungvár became again Uzhhorod, and that Subcarpathia, stripped of any special self-governing status, became the "Transcarpathian oblast of Ukraine."

On November 13, 1944, posters were put up in the cities, towns, villages of Subcarpathia announcing that all ethnic Hungarian and German men between the ages of eighteen and fifty must report for a three-day communal work-duty. This was the infamous *malenkaia robota* (so-called small work detail). More than forty thousand Hungarian men and several thousand Germans gathered and were taken away—not for three days, but for several years to the Gulag. The ethnic cleansing was efficient: only about a third of them returned many years later, most of them in broken health. Many of them did not even reach the Gulag. In the reception camp at nearby Svaliava (Szolyva) a typhoid epidemic broke out. The hundreds of corpses were buried in such a hurry that after heavy rainfalls there have been new outbreaks of typhoid at Svaliava to this very day.

In Subcarpathia, destroyed by the war, all private and municipial property was taken into state ownership: factories, workshops, forests, and stores. The collectivization of agriculture began immediately. Peasants and tradesmen who failed to "volunteer" to join the "cooperatives" were taken to prison camps. The former civil servants, teachers, and intellectuals who did not flee from Subcarpathia were also deported to the northernmost camps of the Gulag. The Soviets crushed the churches: the Greek Catholic, the Roman Catholic and the Protestant churches alike. Their priests also ended up in the Gulag. The terror prevailed until the death of Stalin in 1953. It was after that that the surviving prisoners started to return home one by one.

Culture also fell prey to purging. Official committees revised library collections, and irreplaceable books were sent by the cartload to be pulped. Only elementary schools were allowed to operate in Hungarian. The Rusyns were forced to study in Ukrainian. There was a brief thaw under Khrushchev's reign, e.g., Hungarian high schools were also allowed to open, but the thaw lasted only until Brezhnev came to power.

Subcarpathia had been traditionally a multiethnic, multicultural area. Hungarians have populated this territory since the Hungarian conquest in 895. When I arrived in Uzhhorod in Czechoslovak times, the Hungarian population of Subcarpathia numbered about one hundred thirty thousand. During the decades of Soviet and Ukrainian rule, however, only some small towns and villages have managed to preserve their Hungarian culture. Whereas in 1941 three quarters of the citizens of Uzhhorod and more than half of the citizens of Mukachevo were Hungarians, now the Hungarian population is less than ten percent in both cities.

The largest ethnic group of Subcarpathia is formed by the Rusyns, who populate the Carpathian mountains. Their number is close to a million. Since the Rusyn language is fairly similar to Ukrainian, the existence of a Rusyn nationality different from Ukrainian has not been accepted by the Soviet and Ukrainian authorities, and Rusyn has been declared to be a dialect of Ukrainian. The possibly indigenous Slavic population of the western slopes of the Carpathian mountains, mixed with Lithuanians, Romanians, and farmhands brought in from Galicia and Ukraine, had developed a Rusyn identity by the eighteenth century. Their national identity different from Ukrainian was strengthened by the fact that from the seventeenth century on they were Greek Catholics, following the rites of the Eastern Church but accepting the authority of the Pope. It is no wonder that the Greek Catholic Church was persecuted in Soviet times perhaps even more severely than other religions, and was banned up to December, 1989.

Jews have been present in the region since the tenth century. They have become a significant ethnic group since the middle of the nineteenth century. Subcarpathia was the first stop of the Galician Jewry on their migration to the West; many of them also settled here. Between the two World Wars more than 100,000 Jews lived in this area. Two months after the German occupation of Hungary in 1944, the Subcarpathian Jews were collected in ghettoes and then deported. Only about forty thousand people returned from the Holocaust. The remaining Jewish community was dispersed by Soviet anti-Semitism. From the fifties on, Jews were forced into emigration under the terms "family-unification," "repatriation," etc. By now the Subcarpathian Jewry has practically disappeared.

Saxons (Germans) were also present in large numbers in Subcarpathia from the twelfth century on. Their presence had influenced the culture and architecture of several Subcarpathian towns. A large part of the Jews immigrating from Galicia to Subcarpathia were also German-speaking. It was the Germans who were most severely persecuted by the Soviet authorities. Every Saxon of a working age was taken away to the Gulag. Few of them survived, and afterwards even fewer have dared to call themselves Germans openly.

Whereas the former Subcarpathia had no Russian or Ukrainian population, the Soviet times have brought in masses of Russian-speaking apparatchiks and industrial workers. Most of them, however, are people who have lost their roots and cultural traditions. Many of them are not even Russians, but are people separated from their own national communities in the Caucasus, Central Asia, or the Ural region by the great Soviet migration.

When I arrived in Subcarpathia, it was a multiethnic region where ethnic groups lived in great harmony. Everybody had his or her place and task in that world. The middle class was flourishing. It was appropriate for a bride to arrive here with silverware and evening dresses. An exciting, colorful culture fell prey to the Soviet system, and it is highly questionable whether any of it can be revived after fifty years of destruction and in the present economic and moral crisis. Only the beauty of the Carpathians has been left almost untouched.

CHAPTER 6

The Laszotas, my future husband's family, were all citizens of Uzhhorod, and Sanyi was also born there in 1912. The Laszota family was not rich, but they were considered well-to-do. They had a large house and a harness-making workshop where his father worked with one employee. He started his working day at five a.m. and did not stop until lunch. After lunch he had an hour's rest in his slumbering chair and continued to work until seven p.m. He worked the same hours winter and summer. He never had a vacation. Sanyi also learned his father's trade and worked a month in the family workshop every summer. He was paid the same wages as his father's other employee. Then he was free for the second month of the summer holidays and had money in his pocket.

Sanyi's mother, Veronika Ricza, or for family members, Mamuka, came from the nearby village of Zemplénagárd, which remained under Hungarian sovereignty after World War I. When during the war we had to obtain certificates about our ancestry, it turned out that her birth certificate contained the name "Riczó," which is a Slavic name. Her family must have been Rusyn before it became Hungarian. Mamuka was a Greek Catholic and spoke Rusyn well. She completed eight classes in a Hungarian-Rusyn school. She could express herself perfectly in Hungarian, she picked her words carefully, her spelling was impeccable, and her handwriting was beautiful. Her mother, Sanyi's maternal grandmother, also had a Slavic name: Mária Kótul. She worked as a cook at the Greek Catholic Episcopate. She spoke only Hungarian. In fact, Sanyi's paternal great-great grandfather was also a Slav. He came from Northern Silesia, the neighborhood of Bohumin, from a Polish-Moravian-Slovak family. He was a watchmaker. Sanyi's grandfather, Imre Laszota, considered himself a Hungarian already. His father, József Laszota, could not speak any Slavic language well. He mixed up the gender of words and had problems with grammar. My husband's grand-parents and their siblings all lived very long, but his parents died in their early seventies. They must have been worn out by the cataclysms of history. My Sanyi, fortunately, has lived to be eighty five. His sister is now eighty six, and both of them are in excellent health!

In those days most well-to-do citizens of Uzhhorod had their houses built on their lot in such a way that in addition to the house looking to the street, in which they lived with their families, they also had another house built in the courtyard with apartments to let. Although rents were low, they provided a safe source of subsistence for the owner, espe-cially in his old age when he could not work any longer. My husband's parents also had a backyard at 49 Kapos Street with three undetached houses in a row, plus a fourth house in the middle of the lot. They were rented to Jewish families: the Malermans, the Maisels, the Leizerovitses, and the Moskovitses. A daughter of one of these families still lives in Kapos Street. The others were either deported and killed during the war, or they fled from Uzhhorod.

As a kid, Sanyi spent most of his time with his friends on the banks of the Uzh. They would play there, wrestle, swim across the river, or smear warm mud on themselves. His family did not have much of a social life; they lived according to strict Puritan traditions. Young peo-ple gathered on Sundays in the Catholic and the Protestant Young Men's Club, where they would dance to Gypsy music and to gramophone records. It was there that my Sanyi grew into such an excellent dancer! The men belonging to the Catholic and the Protestant Young Men's Clubs were Hungarians, but they were on good terms with young men of other religions and other nationalities, as well. Hostilities or con-flicts motivated by religious or national differences were absolutely unknown among them. They could speak each other's languages, and they often passed the time together.

Sanyi completed the first three grades in a Rusyn elementary school where both the pupils and the teacher were Hungarians, so no wonder they mostly conversed in their mother tongue. From the fourth grade, Sanyi attended a real Hungarian school, the Roman Catholic Elemen-tary School in Dugonics Street, despite the fact that he was a Lutheran. He was an excellent student. He could continue his studies only in a Rusyn high school (in a so-called *gymnasium*), so at that time it was indispensable for him to learn Rusyn really well. The summer preced-ing high school he devoted to acquiring a mastery of Rusyn. The son of a widowed friend of Mamuka's undertook the task of teaching Sanyi the complicated Rusyn declensions in all three genders, and everything else. At that time there was no standardized literary Rusyn yet, and teaching took place in the local dialect. The teachers at Sanyi's high school included Slovaks, Hungarians, Ukrainians, and also Russians. The principal and the teachers of Ukrainian language and literature were Ukrainians from Galicia. The teachers of mathematics and geography were Hungarians, but they all taught in Rusyn, the official language at that time. The students were also mixed: Rusyns, Hungarians, Czechs, Ukrainians, Jews. From the first year of high school, they studied Latin, Czech, and literary Ukrainian; from the third year, French; and from the fifth year, Russian. They acquired a wide range of knowledge there. Sanyi sat next to Lajcsi Koppelmann throughout the eight years of high school, and they have been best friends to this very day. Sanyi's class graduated in 1931. In the graduation photo they all show off wearing nice moustaches or beards. Unfortunately, we do not have the photo anymore. It fell prey to the war.

The type of school that Sanyi attended, the so-called *gymnasium*, was the most respected of all types of high schools. A person who graduated from a *gymnasium* was held in much higher esteem than someone who graduated from a teachers' training school. Even so, Sanyi later also acquired a teacher's diploma from a teachers' training school because he needed a profession. The *gymnasium* did not qualify him for a career.

After graduation, his parents asked him what profession he intended to choose. It was decided that Sanyi would study law in Bratislava (Pozsony) with the help of his sister and her husband. He began his studies, this time in Slovak. He bought all the expensive books, but he attended law school only for three months. Then there arrived a summons from Prague to the Subcarpathian youths studying in Bratislava and Prague asking them to return to their home region where there were not enough teachers. It said they were needed as Rusyn teachers to educate their people in Rusyn. Sanyi complied; he arrived home on December 15, he submitted his papers to the educational administration on December 16, and on December 17 a courier arrived with the message that he should immediately start teaching at Irliava (Ungsasfalva).

As a non-qualified assistant master, he worked in many different places. Assistant masters were sent to the deepest recesses of the region. They went wherever they were needed. Two years later, in 1931, Sanyi passed the supplementary examinations for the teachers' diploma, this time in Russian because the teachers' training school in Mukachevo operated in Russian. (For Sanyi, fortunately, it is completely natural to use different languages and always to switch to the language which is needed at the given moment. Of the many languages he speaks, French is the only one in which he is not completely fluent because he has never had an opportunity to practice it.) He had to pass a supplementary exam in three subjects: didactics, pedagogy, and music. The exams were followed by a demonstration lesson at the training school of the teacher training institute. The committee selected a topic which Sanyi had to teach to a class. Given that he had had two years of practice before, teaching was not a problem for him, and he received a good grade.

A teacher earned around one thousand crowns, and a single teacher got a room in a town house and full board for three hundred crowns. Everything was very cheap, from Batya shoes to food. One could live very well on a teacher's salary. Often both husband and wife were teachers, and their combined salaries made a really comfortable standard of living possible. We were first two, then three, and finally four to provide for, but nevertheless we did not lack anything. To be sure, we also raised chickens and ducks at home.

In those days a teacher taught everything, and to more than one class at the same time. In small elementary schools divided into two or three groups, Sanyi usually got the upper classes, because female teachers found it more difficult to discipline bigger children. There were many woman teachers already, even if it was not a completely feminine profession yet. My husband taught in very poor villages. Even so, quite a number of his pupils got into a *gymnasium*, and became civil servants in a notary's office or clerks at the forest directorate. To his great pride, some of his pupils even became lawyers, teachers, or principals! It is beyond imagination what this meant to a destitute family of a poverty-stricken Rusyn village. Therefore, the teacher of a village was in great esteem, and not only in his own village. Teachers, in general, had a high rank in society.

As a teacher, Sanyi was allowed to postpone his military service for years. In 1935 he was finally called up to do service in the Czech army. From his first barracks in Moravia he was immediately sent on to an officers' training corps in Olomouc. In the Czech army everybody who had graduated from a high school was sent on an officers' training course. The course was not easy for Sanyi because its language was Czech, and although he had studied in four languages by that time, Czech was not among them. Moreover, he was not very motivated because he did not intend to remain in the army. Nevertheless, once he had an opportunity to advance, he took advantage of it. It makes a difference whether one performs one's military service as a GI or an officer. After spending a year at the officers' training corps and obtaining the rank of officer, Sanyi served for another year in Kroměříž, a town in Moravia. There an interesting thing happened to him. A major, knowing that Sanyi was a teacher, asked him to perform a special duty. He had to teach illiterate boys from villages hidden in the forests of the Carpathian mountains to read and write. His class consisted of fifteen Hungarian and Jewish boys, whom he taught for six months—in Hungarian, in the Czech army, in the middle of Moravia! Each one of them learned to read and write. We still have a photo in which Sanyi sits among his pupils. He was discharged from the army in the fall of 1937.

Immediately after my arrival in Uzhhorod, my future mother-in-law took me to Kroměříž, to visit my fiancé. We had to travel quite a distance! Our first meeting was thrilling! I knew right away that I had not come to Europe in vain! We stayed there for one week, and Sanyi got permission from his commander to go out every single day of the week. We spent the whole day together; he only had to return to the barracks for the night.

The habits and principles prevailing in the Czech army were humane in other respects, as well. The official date of discharge was October 31. Knowing that Sanyi was a teacher, he was dismissed on August 31 so that he could start teaching the next day. This way his military service lasted only for twenty-two months, instead of two years. This was automatically arranged by the army; we did not even have to request it.

On the first day of September, 1937, Sanyi was already teaching in Turia Bystra (Hungarian: Turjabisztra), 50 kilometers to the northeast of Uzhhorod.

CHAPTER 7

My settling in Uzhhorod was not so unclouded as the week we spent in Kroměříž. There is no denying it: I cried a lot. It was then that I realized what I had done. There I was all by myself in an alien world, in which there existed no bathroom, no flush toilet, no vacuum cleaner, no refrigerator. In principle I knew what the circumstances would be like, but I never really thought about what this would imply for my everyday life. When we had been in Uzhhorod before, these had been Mommy's problems. We little girls were not let into housekeeping or into other matters of adults. In those days children were not familiar with family problems. Even at dinner parties they were seated at a separate children's table. In Uzhhorod everything proved to be more complicated and at the same time also more Puritan that what I had been used to at home. Everything was very, very different!

I began my new life in my sister-in-law's household, subjected to her control, unable to defend myself. She did not even allow me to play tennis, although I had brought along my tennis rackets from America. She showed herself very different from the woman we had gotten to know when we had been in Uzhhorod together with Mommy. She welcomed me with the same exuberant affection with which she had said good-bye to me three years before. Slowly I realized, however, that this affection was different from what I thought it to be.

When her friends were visiting, she sent me out to work in the kitchen while they were having a good time together. This was very strange to me; in our home things went differently! What is more, she would repeat to her visitors: "Mary does not know this, Mary does not know that!" I was aware of the fact that I had to learn housekeeping, but not in that way!

I got to Uzhhorod right from school, and would have liked to continue studying. "You don't need that!" my future sister-in-law used to say. "Your diploma is the rolling-pin!" She did not even allow me to finish my thesis which I had begun at home, even though I had promised I would send it back completed. A Ukrainian family renting an apartment in our backyard offered to teach me Ukrainian in exchange for my teaching their child English, so it would not have cost me anything. My sister-in-law did not allow me to do that either! I was put up in her home; she could dictate to me! She had stopped studying after the eighth grade. Nevertheless, she was a well-read, cultured, society woman, who could even discuss politics. She liked to be the center of things and to dominate over those who let her. I let her! And my Sanyi was still serving in the army.

I was so much in love with Sanyi that I resigned myself to everything, quietly, longing for home. Only God knew when I was crying. Anyway, I had brought all that on myself. When I met my sister in 1981, she asked me how I could have endured all that. Well, if we love someone very much, we can endure everything. I would not trade my Sanyi for an easier, richer life!

During the three years that passed between my two journeys to Uzhhorod, my sister-in-law and her husband bought the Moncsák house, the one in which both they and we had rented an apartment. They were running a thriving general store not far from the house. In the Moncsák house there was room to set up a bigger store, and that was why they wanted to buy it. The Moncsák family were just about to have a new house built, so they were glad to sell off the old one. The new location proved to be ideal for the store. The whole Greek Catholic neighborhood, including the teacher training school and the episcopate, did their shopping there. The railway station, the basilica, the forest directorate, the botanical gardens, and the high school were also close to the store and brought lots of shoppers. The store had a huge turnover.

As we found out later, my sister-in-law and her husband bought the Moncsák house with the help of a loan of 7,000 dollars (equivalent to 60,000 crowns) borrowed from my parents. They promised to pay the sum back in dollars. Since I moved to Uzhhorod, my parents decided that the 7,000 dollars to be repaid should be mine, and until it was returned I should receive the monthly interest. As I did not work, the interest meant my monthly income. I was paid the interest in kind, in the form of goods from the store. Since it was a store stocked with everything, we found whatever we needed there from sliced ham to chocolate.

The loan turned out to have been a mistake. After a while problems arose with the interest payments, and the original capital was never repaid. In this the ensuing historical turmoil also had a role. The fact that my sister-in-law never paid up outraged my father so much that he broke off all correspondence with all of the Laszotas, including Sanyi. Mommy liked Sanyi very much, and they were close to each other until circumstances dictated otherwise. Nevertheless, she also concluded that my sister-in-law deceived us. When she came to Uzhhorod in 1965, after twenty three years, she happily renewed all her old acquaintances. My sister-in-law was the only one whom she refused to meet.

Sanyi found out about the loan much later. It hurt and annoyed him very much. Still he was convinced that his sister supported our marriage, and not only because she hoped to derive financial benefit from it. But whatever her motives were, our marriage was, and has always been, a match made from love.

As I said, I spent my engagement time as a "guest" of my sister-in-law. For her "hospitality" she charged my parents 1000 crowns a month—at a time when one could get a room with full board, washing, etc., for 300 crowns a month. In any case, she entertained me generously: I arrived in Uzhhorod a frail, skinny little girl, and she fed me into a big, stout woman—which Sanyi did not mind at all.

By the time I arrived in Uzhhorod, the new store had been completed and had already opened. The house was not supplied with modern conveniences yet. This happened only after the war. We washed ourselves in a washbowl with a sponge in a part of the kitchen. Each of us knew when it was his or her turn to use it. There were three outhouses in the courtyard; these we used as toilets. We brought water from a well in the middle of the courtyard. My sister-in-law and her husband had three rooms which opened onto each other. Fortunately, the innermost room was mine, so it was me who passed through them, and not the other way around.

My sister-in-law was an excellent cook. We spent every morning together in the kitchen. Poor Mommy was shocked when, coming to our wedding, she caught sight of my hands. In theory, I was slaving in the kitchen in order to learn everything about housekeeping. In fact, what was left to me was peeling, cleaning, cutting up, grinding, whipping, and stirring. Practicing these did not make me an independent cook. I was too busy with the drudgery to learn the crucial phases of cooking.

Weekdays began with going to the market. My sister-in-law did the shopping herself, even though she had two helpers. Two very nice women, Zsuzsika and Rózsika, came to the house on alternate days. Each worked two days a week. One did the washing and ironing, and the other the cleaning. Shopping, on the other hand, "could not be left to someone else."

My sister-in-law had her dresses made, so we often called in at the shops to have a look at the new materials, and often dropped in at the hatter, too. She was treated with great reverence everywhere, and was a well-known lady of fashion. She took me along wherever she went, but I could not go without her anywhere except to the house of my future parents-in-laws.

I had friends in Uzhhorod from when I went to school there for eight months: Rózsika Gergely; Edit Klein, after whom my granddaughter Edit was named; Ibolya Katz, who unfortunately did not return from a concentration camp; and two sisters, Kati and Zsuzsi Bán. While I was staying with my sister-in-law I was not allowed to visit them, and they could not come to see me either because allegedly it was not becoming of a fiancée. It was not becoming to play tennis, go to the movies, go for a walk with my girlfriends, or even talk with them! It was my sister-in-law who took me to the movies from time to time. She practically monopolized me! I could never get used to that, but I put up with it. I saw no other way.

My American friends wrote to me sometimes. They sent me photos, but I did not answer them. I felt there was no point to it. Of my former life it was my parents alone with whom I maintained contact. I did not even correspond with my sister. After I became independent I also started a correspondence with my cousin, Margó.

I spent every Thursday with Sanyi's parents. My mother-in-law proved to be more compliant than my sister-in-law. On the days I spent at their place I was allowed to make friends with their tenants from the courtyard. Mamuka also had visitors who came to see her together with their young relations, with whom we could pass the time very well. In general, there was a more liberal atmosphere there. I did not feel so much locked up behind closed doors. Thursday was already a better day, and then soon came Saturday, when my dear arrived!

After his discharge Sanyi managed to get a job in a village close to Uzhhorod, but we could not spend much time together even after that. He could come to Uzhhorod only for the weekends and had to leave already on Sunday afternoon. Turia Bystra, the village where he taught, was about fifty kilometers in the northeast of Uzhhorod, and could only be reached in a complicated way: one had to take a train to Perechyn (Hungarian: Perecseny) and take a bus there. Turia Bystra was a large Greek Catholic village with a church, a kindergarten, and four schools, each employing several teachers. The doctor went up to the village only once a week. When some urgent medical problem came up, people had to go to the neighboring village of Poroshkovo (Poroskő). The Bauntin factory had a division in Turia Bystra, so the village also had a German community which remained there even after the factory ceased to operate.

This was the place where my Sanyi spent the week, waiting for Saturday to come. In the afternoon I always met him at the railway station in a flutter, dressed and made up beautifully. When Sanyi arrived, we dropped in on his sister and went to see his parents. Mamuka treated us to a delicious dinner, after which my fiancé saw me home. There we passed some time together still. Playing cards was very much in fashion, and we, too, played "jolly seven" and similar games. At other times we played dominoes or just listened to the radio. In an engagement basically nothing was allowed, but we were happy just to see each other! Finally, Sanyi went back to his parents' to sleep. Our Sunday mornings were spent similarly, except that they also included going to church and promenading. In the afternoon I saw him off at the station.

From the station I usually returned to Mamuka's, and the three of us went to the movies together. They also loved movies, and in Uzhhorod lots of good films were shown. The movie program differed from what American movies offered only in that besides the Hollywood hits excellent Hungarian films were also run. My favorites were the ice-skating films of Sonia Henny. If a Sonia Henny film was on, Mamuka sent Papa for me, and we went to see it right away. Papa visited me every day, and the dear, old, gallant gentleman always arrived with a rose for me. He tried to please me in every possible way. My sister-in-law remarked that she had never received flowers from her father. Papa loved films as much as I did. What a pity he did not live to see television! After our Sunday movies they saw me home and then trotted home themselves.

My week of loneliness started again. There were no visible conflicts around me; I simply could not be quarrelled with! If I had to defend myself, the words would have stuck in my throat. I acted quietly, but bitterness was building up inside me. It happened more than once that I asked my fiancé to help me pack because I was going home. I cried and cried, and I could not even explain to Sanyi why. Sanyi merely asked me: "Could you leave me, could you forsake me?" Well, I could not. Our Saturdays made me conscious of why I endured everything, why I was there, no matter how the week passed. I chose him. I loved him.

It was the fall of 1937.

CHAPTER 8

O ur engagement lasted as long as it did because we were waiting for Mommy. She brought the bridal gown and the other accessories, and in addition to that, also an incredible amount of other presents for all of us. With the bridal gown, however, there were problems. My sister-in-law's ambition was to feed and fatten up everybody around her. She was very successful in my case. When Mommy arrived in May, and caught sight of me, she threw up her hands in astonishment: "You won't fit into your wedding dress, little elephant!" I had to go on a diet. I went up to the little village where Sanyi taught, and did not eat anything but yoghurt for ten days. That was how I eventually managed to squeeze into my dress.

With no other hindrance to our marriage left, the day of our wedding was named: July 2nd, Saturday for the civil wedding, and the following day, Sunday, for the church ceremony. The civil wedding took place at the registrar's office. The marriage certificate was written in Czech, and it includes the sentence that "the wife, Mary Halász, is an American citizen who does not renounce her American citizenship in marriage." I still have this certificate! I have not given up my American citizenship since then either, so I have been an American citizen to this very day.

We had our church ceremony in a Roman Catholic church. Sanyi, who is a Lutheran, had to concede that the girls issuing from our marriage would be Roman Catholic, whereas the boys would be Lutheran. So it happened.

The so-called "witnesses" to our marriage, i.e., the person to give me away and Sanyi's best man, were our brothers-in-law, both in dinner jackets made to order. My sister-in-law also showed up very elegantly in a black dress so fashionable at that time. Mommy, too, had new dresses made for the occasion: a gala dress for the church ceremony and a two-piece black suit for the civil marriage. At that time she was a striking, buxom, 38-year-old lady, and she attracted great attention. The photographer remarked: "The bride is lovely, so is her attire, but her mother is even more beautiful." That was his wedding gift for me!

My wedding gown was a skin-tight, shiny satin dream dress, with a lace inlet at the neck and the sleeves, with tiny buttons, and a long train carried by two little girls. The wonderful underwear, including a one-piece corset, as well as the other accessories were all of the same quality, prepared of the same material. The twelve-meter-long veil, fastened to a wreath made of the material of the dress, was folded into the train, and was fully opened only in the church. The veil was decorated in its full length with tiny myrtles, and was, therefore, extremely difficult to iron. It was made of tulle as thin as a spider's web. I did use it for that later on! I would always cut a piece of it for our pram so that our babies should not be bothered by mosquitoes and flies. My dress was later recut for the First Communion of a little girl in the family. I am glad that it was put to use somehow. It would have been more painful if my wedding gown and veil had also been destroyed like everything else that we had.

Our church wedding followed the script of local traditions. Family members were to arrive at the church first, and the bride was to arrive last together with the witnesses. The bridegroom was to wait for the bride at the door of the church. Well, the cab which was to take me to the church broke down! That was how things started! Eventually the cab jolted there somehow, but it took at least half an hour. When the wedding procession got to the church without the bride, everybody thought I must have run away.

While the civil ceremony at the registrar's office was attended only by the close family, the whole city was present at the church. The Laszota family was one of the best-known, most respected old families of Uzhhorod. Furthermore, the news spread that Sanyi Laszota had brought a wife from America, and everybody wanted to see me! All in all, it was a spectacular, great wedding, followed by a dinner for sixty. The dinner party was held in my sister-in-law's house, in the three rooms opening onto each other. The guests were made up of relatives and friends. From my side, only Mommy and Uncle András Halász from Leles were present. The Uzhhorod relatives and our friends had to be invited personally. Since Sanyi only came home for the weekends, it took a while before we could visit everyone. Fortunately, there weren't

46

any great distances in Uzhhorod, so we could cram two or three visits into one afternoon.

A traditional element of weddings was the dance with the bride at midnight. At the end of it the husband catches her up and runs away with her. The dance was usually started by the best man shouting: "The bride is for sale!" This signalled that the male guests were to pay for a dance with her. The money collected this way in the best man's hat usually covered a significant part of the expenses of the wedding feast. Mommy did not allow a "bride's sale," but we received lovely, valuable wedding presents anyway: crystals, porcelain dinner sets, a wonderful Chinese tea service, cooking dishes, tablecloths, all kinds of beautiful things that could be used in a new household.

It would not have been worthwhile to carry heavy wedding presents from America. American household appliances wouldn't have been of any use anyway, since we had no electricity in Turia Bystra. Therefore my American relatives, Margó's parents, and my cousins, sent us money. US dollars were worth a lot in those days, too. I spent them on bedcovers and curtains, among other things.

The wedding dinner was organized in an elegant and convenient way. Everything was catered; nothing was prepared at home. Mr. Miskolczi, the best confectioner in Uzhhorod, whose shop was very close to our place, took care of everything; things only had to be warmed up at home. Mr. Miskolczi undertook to prepare not only the cakes but the whole meal, including the meats and the sauces. He also brought along the dinner set, the cutlery, the serving dishes, together with two elegant waiters. Miskolczi's speciality was catering for weddings.

The feast began at five p.m. I was too excited to eat anything, but I still remember the menu. It began with a boullion served in cups, then continued with boiled meat served with sauces, which was followed by stuffed cabbage and stacked cabbage, then roasted and fried meats, stuffed chickens, assorted cold meats and salads, pastries and biscuits, and finally the wonderful cakes. Given that Mr. Miskolczi was a confectioner by profession, his cakes were particularly amazing. There were all kinds of drinks: brandys, liqueurs, among them the famous Hungarian Unicum and Hubertus, as well as wines, champagnes, and lots of soda water.

Sanyi and I were sitting at the head of the large U-shaped table, and were waiting for the time to come when we could disappear. Following the tradition, after a while I changed into a "new wife's dress," a pretty silk dress with a pleated skirt, which I used afterwards as a Sunday outfit.

Parfait was to be the last course. I had always loved ice cream, so I thought a little cold stuff would certainly go down my throat. I was really counting on it. The parfait was just about to be served when the best man announced that it was midnight. The dance with the bride was to begin. I danced as long as it was becoming, and then the young husband "abducted" me. Before the parfait!

Mamuka furnished a room for us in their house; that was the place to which I was "abducted." A cab, which was on permanent service during the wedding, drove us to Mamuka's house. We agreed with the driver that in the morning he would come and drive us to the railway station since we were going on our honeymoon by train. We had already packed our suitcases. We were spending our honeymoon at Bardejovské Kúpele, a famous quiet little spa near the town of Bardejov (Bártfa) in northeastern Slovakia. The cabdriver allegedly showed up indeed, and was knocking at the door for a long time, but we did not hear him.

I was very much exhausted by the wedding, but I was also slightly afraid, and anyway I did not want to spend our wedding night at Mamuka's house. My considerate and understanding Sanyi accepted that. I tumbled onto the bed without even taking off my clothes, and fell asleep immediately. Sanyi must have been sleeping soundly, too, since he was not wakened by the cab driver's loud knocking either. The driver was pounding for a while, then gave up and went home. We woke up late, just as Sanyi's parents arrived home from the wedding. "What are you doing here? Has Jóska not come for you?" they asked. Sanyi ran to the cab driver's, who lived nearby, to demand an explanation. He just laughed and said he did not want to disturb us too much. By that time we were already as hungry as wolves. My poor father-in-law went back to fetch us some food, but by that time all the leftovers had disappeared. The musicians with all their relatives were scurrying around the tables. Mommy could only collect a few pieces of cake, but it was not what I wanted. At home there was nothing to eat in the store because of the wedding. Finally my mother-in-law made some scrambled eggs for us, then we walked to the railway station. We missed our train again, this time by inches! That was how our life together started: with our train missed twice! We did not risk missing it for the third time. We waited for the next train there at the railway station.

It was late at night when we arrived at Bardejov, but we managed to find a room at a nice hotel. We spent weeks very happy there. We had nothing to care about; we received full board at the hotel. They found out that we were honeymooners, and from the second day on we were seated at a table in a corner, hidden behind a huge bunch of flowers. We took every breakfast, lunch, and dinner at that table. Our hotel suite included a flush toilet, but it had still no bathroom. We washed in a porcelain washbowl.

Time passed very quickly. We took long walks in the huge pine forests surrounding Bardejovské Kúpele. We did not go to the famous thermal baths since we had no rheumatic complaints to alleviate, but we often visited the swimming pool. In the evenings we went dancing. My Sanyi was a famous dancer, admired for his dancing skills at the Sunday parties of the Young Men's Associations and the balls of Uzhhorod's entertainment section: the row of wine cellars. We had a wonderful honeymoon!

CHAPTER 9

I n the third week of our marriage my husband received a call-up order for an abbreviated military training and had to leave. The war had not broken out yet but there were already premonitory signs. Mamuka took me to a little spa since I had problems with my stomach and because she thought, that with Sanyi in the army, time would pass easier for me there. Sanyi came home at the end of August, and on the first of September we moved into our first common home in the village where he taught.

Sanyi was appointed to the school of a separate section of Turia Bystra called Svaliavka. He was the only teacher there and taught eight grades simultaneously. We had an apartment in the schoolhouse, and our door was next to the door of the classroom. We had a room, a kitchen, and a pantry—naturally, all without electricity.

The school year began. The villagers were very fond of their schoolmaster. They had known Sanyi beforehand because he often went over to Svaliavka when he taught in the school of Turia Bystra. The villagers were very proud that their master had brought an American wife. They would come to admire me, especially because during the day I wore sports clothes. I found them more convenient for housework.

After a week Mamuka came to visit us, and she stayed for a while. She cooked for us, and in the meantime she taught me everything I needed to know. We cooked on a wood-burning range. Wood was no problem there up in the mountains. We bought wonderful logs separately for ourselves and for the school. We had them only sawed up, because my husband's hobby was wood-splitting. He also liked to arrange the split wood carefully in the woodshed, so our woodshed looked as neat as the pantry of a meticulous housewife. He chopped wood the way we chop onions. We were very much in love and were also happy in the middle of the woods.

A sweet old woman cleaned the school and she also helped me

around the house. If I needed her, I just shouted: "babahooo," and she came running to find out what the "schoolmistress" wanted. Her son, Jancsó, often helped me, too. It was he who brought me water for laundering. Water had to be brought from a fairly great distance. We could buy laundry soap, but it also happened that I boiled some. I always made lye myself from ashes for softening water, despite the fact that we washed with the water of the mountain stream Turia, which was not hard.

Unfortunately, Sanyi received another drafting order at the end of September. The Czech government did not believe that the great powers would yield up the Sudetenland to Germany, and were mobilizing the army to defend it. Sanyi had to join a unit near the German border. They were deployed with their light machine guns, but meanwhile the Munich Pact was signed, and they were ordered to retreat. They surrendered the Sudetenland without firing a shot.

The children of Svaliavka were left without a teacher. Some continued school in Turia Bystra, others stopped going to school altogether. I stayed. After all, the schoolhouse in Svaliavka was my home. Mommy, however, soon came up to collect me. She had not returned to America yet because I was pregnant and she wanted to wait for the birth of her first grandchild. She would not have missed the joy of a new baby in the family for anything! Several decades later I learned from my sister that Daddy endured Mommy's long absence in very poor spirits.

Mommy stayed with my sister-in-law in my former room. They got on well with each other. Mommy's strong personality could not be suppressed. She maintained her former circle of friends, cultivated her social relations, and in general had a great time. When she visited me, we cried for a while, then packed up my personal belongings, closed up everything carefully, and went down to Uzhhorod.

On November 2, 1938, the southern part of Slovakia and Subcarpathia, including Uzhhorod and Mukachevo, were, in accordance with the so-called First Vienna Award, returned to Hungary after nineteen years of Czechoslovak rule. At that time Mommy and I were both staying with my sister-in-law, so we were witnesses to the Hungarian army entering Uzhhorod. It is unimaginable how much it meant to us spiritually. The radio kept announcing that the Hungarians were already approaching, and it also said precisely where they were at any given moment. Many Hungarian families were already sewing Hungarian flags secretly. My sister-in-law must have bought the materials of different colors at different shops, because nobody noticed what she was up to. All of a sudden she drew forth wonderful red, white, and green silks, and Mommy sewed a beautiful Hungarian tricolor of them with a golden braid and golden tassels.

When the radio announced that the Hungarians were about to enter Uzhhorod, we flung the huge shuttered windows open, and hung the flag out. We were the first to put out the Hungarian flag in the whole city, but we were immediately followed by countless people! The governor of Hungary, Miklós Horthy, riding a white horse, was at the head of the troups marching in. Dressed in our best clothes, we ran into the street, and Mommy and my sister-in-law kept hugging and kissing the soldiers. The general enthusiasm also gripped me. I, and the thousands of people celebrating in the streets, were not aware of the fact that the First Vienna Award, which returned Uzhhorod and the southernmost part of Ruthenia to Hungary, was a decision of Nazi Germany and Italy. It was not approved of, let alone guaranteed, by the other of the great powers; hence, it had no chance to be effective for long.

From that day on Sanyi and I did not know anything about each other since he served in Czech territory, whereas we were now under Hungarian sovereignty. So, in my personal life, the entry of the Hungarians meant losing track of my husband and waiting for his return, often in tears.

The Czechs started packing, and their entire administration left. There had been several mixed marriages in Uzhhorod, and many of the mixed families also chose to move. While the Czechs moved out, many Hungarians who had left before came home. A Hungarian administration was set up, and Hungarian IDs and Hungarian passports were issued. These changes did not affect me since I had been, and remained, an American citizen. Neither did the Rusyns working as lumbermen up in the forests of the Carpathian mountains care much about them. They had been living in misery and knew it would not change. In fact, their condition became better in one respect. Under Hungarian rule lumbermen employed in the state forestries were regularly assigned a certain amount of bacon. In general, the change of sovereignty took place quietly and did not upset everyday life.

The Czech army no longer needed the services of men who were from the territories returned to Hungary, therefore Sanyi was discharged at the beginning of December and came home for good. He became a Hungarian citizen and he still has the certificate testifying to it. Our children were born as Hungarian citizens. When they moved to Hungary as adults, they merely had to arrange for their repatriation. When Sanyi returned from the army, the Saliavka school had a different teacher already, so we had to empty the schoolmaster's residence. We had nice, mild weather in December, 1938. We obtained a truck to fetch our belongings. Our wonderful furniture had been carefully kept for us.

Sanyi received a job in Dravtsi (Daróc), a village just three or four kilometers from the center of Uzhhorod. It had a big school divided into classes, with at least seven or eight teachers. Our official residence occupied half of a house in the courtyard of the school. It was so big that we did not use every room. The other half of the house was inhabited by the headmaster and his family. The headmaster's wife, a nice elderly lady, helped me a lot with the household. I used to cook from "Aunt Vilma's cookbook" and "Aunt Margit's cookbook." (I have just given one of them to my daughter. It contains everything, including how to slaughter and prepare a pig.) I remember that as a beginner I had problems with pancakes. They just stuck to the pan, whatever I did. It was the headmaster's wife who showed me how to make pancakes, among many other practical things. Since she lived next door, I could run to her at all times, even between two stirrings, when I needed advice in the kitchen. The rest of the teachers had their own houses in Dravtsi.

Our apartment had four rooms, but we used only two of them. We still had to bring water from a well outside, and we had no electricity either. We cooked and heated with woodburning stoves, so Sanyi could indulge in wood-cutting.

We had moved to Dravtsi in December, 1938, so we celebrated our first Christmas together in our home there. We invited Mommy, one of her friends, the priest who married us, and who was also a relation of ours, and my sister-in-law and her husband. Mommy helped with the cooking, and the cakes and pastries I bought from the never-failing Miskolczi. (Incidentally, I am still in touch with Miskolczi's daughter. Married to a priest, she lives up in the Carpathian mountains. Sometimes we meet and recall the old times with nostalgia.)

We bought a lovely big Christmas tree, and decorated it beautifully, in a mixed European-American style, with glass balls, garlands, fine glass-filaments and candies. At that time everything was still available and we also had the money to buy it.

I cooked the traditional Subcarpathian Christmas menu. The first course was mushroom soup with sauerkraut. Everybody found it delicious. (I have come to like this typical local soup; we often cook it in the summer, too, with mushrooms picked by Sanyi.) The soup was followed by fish, naturally, with mushroom-sauce. Then came the poppyseed noodles. They are made from leavened dough rolls cut up and baked on a baking sheet, then scalded with milk, stacked with layers of ground, sugared poppy seed in a dish, and baked once more.

The dinner was a great success. Everybody seemed to like their presents as well. I only remember the wonderful pajamas I received. Mommy always gave us money, which we were to spend on what we needed the most. Eventually the guests left by cabs ordered in advance.

The doctor prescribed lots of walking for me, so we often went on foot to see Mommy, who was still staying with my sister-in-law. If I was in good shape, we also walked the six kilometer path back home to Dravtsi. If I felt the first six kilometers were enough, Mommy called for a four-wheeler to take us home. I enjoyed these visits in either way. Fortunately, by that time I was over the morning sickness of the first months.

When in Uzhhorod, I regularly went to see my seamstresses: Aranka and Malvin, two nice, skillful Jewish girls working together. I did not find them through my sister-in-law. She had her dresses made by a ladies' tailor with a showroom. Aranka and Malvin had an apartment in the same courtyard as Aunt Annus Klein, and she also had her dresses made by them. I thought if their work satisfied a lady of her taste and status, it would certainly suit me. So it did!

Uzhhorod was so close to us that we could also enjoy its thriving cultural life. Every national community maintained a theater, and we regularly attended the Hungarian performances. We subscribed to a Hungarian daily paper, a magazine, and a women's weekly, which were delivered to us in Dravtsi. We lived a happy, quiet, balanced life, but we were never bored.

CHAPTER 10

W e remained in Dravtsi only until the middle of April. I was more and more often overcome by vicious coughing fits, and the doctors had no idea what precipitated them. They thought the clear mountain air might help, and suggested that we move up higher in the Carpathians. Sanyi asked to be transferred to Perechyn (Hungarian: Perecseny) or Turia Bystra, and in the meantime we returned to Uzhhorod temporarily, where we moved into a cozy little house with one room, a kitchen, a pantry, and a veranda, in the courtyard of my sister-in-law.

Sanyi was offered a job in Simer (Ószemere), just three kilometers to the east of Perechyn. He commuted there every day. He took a train to Perechyn, then switched to a bicycle which he kept there, and pedaled on to Simer.

In Uzhhorod we had a neighbor who was running a catering business, and we ordered lunch from him every day. His portions were so large that they sufficed for supper as well, so I only had to provide breakfast for us. We lived a beautiful, easy life and could devote a lot of time to each other.

During the day, while Sanyi was away, Mommy and I went downtown to do some shopping. Thanks to Mommy, we bought wonderful baby things, among them a cot. The godparents bought a beautiful, padded pram, as was customary in those days. The baby was due around the 30th of April. My husband had already prepared our future home in Simer, but since I needed medical care, I was going to move up to the mountains only after the delivery, together with the baby.

It was the 23rd of April, a Sunday, Mamuka's fiftieth birthday. We celebrated the eve of her birthday. On Saturday the whole family gathered for a festive dinner. Although I had never been a great eater, at that dinner I ate for three. Both Mommy and Sanyi warned me that I would be sick in the end. When we went home, I already felt very ill. Sanyi ran for Mommy, who first blamed my sickness on my gluttony! But then she realized that the problem was of a different nature; my water had broken. She called for a cab, and we went to the midwives' training institute, which was fortunately nearby.

At four o'clock on Sunday, on Mamuka's fiftieth birthday, her first grandchild was born: a little girl, Lia. After my own heart I would have given her a different name: Eleonóra, Nórika. Aurélia was picked by my sister-in-law. Since she was her godmother, she was entitled—more precisely, she felt herself entitled—to decide the baby's name. Later, however, I found that Lia, Liácska sounded cute, and reconciled myself to her choice.

My sister-in-law had a phone, so it was she whom the doctor called up with the good news. He told me afterwards that there was such loud cheering at the other end of the phone as is only given to boys in other families. At first I was not allowed to receive visitors because it had been a difficult delivery with forceps since the umbilical cord had been twisted around the neck of the baby. Only my husband and my brother-in-law were let in. Nobody else was allowed to disturb me.

My Sanyi arrived home very sad after his visit. At first he did not want to say why, but then he admitted that something was wrong with the baby. When Mommy questioned him further, he eventually blurted out that the baby was born with two heads! He even drew a picture of a baby with a head on top of which another head grew out! The whole family was beside themselves with grief, and could not wait for the morning to come when they could see the baby.

As the youngest mother at the hospital with the smallest baby, I received special treatment, and I had a room for just the two of us. I was still under nineteen, and little Lia only weighed five pounds. Everybody knew about us, because our data were written on a board in the corridor. From time to time people would come and peek in to see us.

In the morning, Mommy was our first visitor. She took the baby in her hands, and her comment was: "This is the most beautiful baby I have ever seen, but it is very strange that she seems to have two heads." She talked with the doctor, who reassured her that the forceps stretched the apparent second head, and by the time we went home, the baby's head would be perfectly round. So it happened. I was let home after nine days, with an impeccable-looking girl.

Unfortunately, I barely had any milk. What was more, Lia was born a fickle baby; she did not accept either the feeding bottle or the spoon. Consequently, she was perpetually hungry and constantly cried. She naturally did not put on as much weight as she should have. We bought the best baby food, but there was no way to get it into her. In the end I laid her on the table, and Papa started to play the violin. My little Lia—who must have been fond of music at that early age already—gaped with astonishment, and I immediately put a little spoonful of food into her mouth. Unfortunately, she also spat out most of the food we tricked her into eating that way, so I was desperate.

Lia's non-eating period lasted a long time, and could not be helped either by the doctor or by the midwife. I tried everything. For instance, I sugared, then honeyed the nipple of the bottle, but in vain! After we went home from the hospital, I spent my days in preparing food for the baby, and always alert to the possibility that perhaps there would come a suitable moment when I could trick a drop into her mouth. As long as Mommy was in Uzhhorod with us, she did everything else: she bathed the baby, washed and ironed her clothes, etc. I only had to care about feeding her, and Papa took care of playing the violin. For Mommy it was very hard to part with her granddaughter, but she could not postpone going home much longer. Daddy was growing more and more impatient, and the outer conditions also compelled her to leave. In the tense political situation more and more often foreign citizens were expelled. She left when my little Lia was three months old. We saw her again only after twenty-three years!

I soon got the knack for babycare myself, so we found it was time to leave Uzhhorod. We were given a very nice residence in Perechyn, in a very good location. My coughing, however, worsened and became stranger and stranger. The doctors suspected it might be whooping cough, but it ought to have ceased after a while. They thought of hayfever, as well, but that diagnosis also proved to be wrong when it turned out that I was coughing in every season: winter and summer, spring and fall. In Perechyn there was a large acetone factory, and it seemed possible that it contributed to the worsening of my condition. It was suggested that we should go still higher, where the air was still cleaner. So after one year in Perechyn, we moved on again. The beginning of the school year found us in Turia Bystra again. This time Sanyi found a job in a school with six teachers in the center of the village.

Turia Bystra is fifty-four kilometers from Uzhhorod. It was easily reached: an entrepreneur ran a bus between Turia Bystra and the

Perechyn railway station twice a day, for 10 crowns in the Czech era, and for one and a half *pengő* in Hungarian times. When we moved up, I was already heavily pregnant with my son. We had a beautiful, warm fall that year. In a photo where we are already sitting with the new baby, little Lia is still wearing a light summer dress. Öcsi ("little brother" in Hungarian) was due to be born on October 28th. When our time had come, I went with Lia down to Uzhhorod. My sister-in-law was to look after her during the few days I was supposed to be in the hospital. Quite a number of days went by actually, but Öcsi was still not born! I felt sorry for my husband left alone for such a long time, although in fact our maid was with him.

Our maid's name was originally Olenka, but our children called her Nenuka. Nenuka was a girl from Turia Bystra, and since she had no family and no relatives, she stayed with us. She had a fold-up bed with a wire mattress in our kitchen. We were exactly of the same age. Naturally, we treated her as a member of the family. She had her meals with us, and we did all the housework together. I taught her to knit and to darn. In the evenings we did needlework together by the light of the paraffin lamp. I taught Nenuka to wash and dress herself properly, and to take care of herself during her period. It was me who first put panties and stockings on her! From that time on, I gave her underwear as presents for every occasion. I also had pretty flannel and corduroy dresses made for her. On weekdays she wore the dresses that she got from me, but on holidays she always put on her national costume; that was how she went to the Greek Catholic mass. She was a kind, complaisant girl, and she was absolutely reliable. It was she who looked after Sanyi while we were staying in Uzhhorod.

By the first of November I could not wait any longer. I packed up, took Lia by the hand, and we went home, saying: let the baby come whenever he wants to! After travelling by train and by bus, we still had a long way to walk, but we met acquaintances from Turia Bystra who helped us, so we made it home safely. We were quite a surprise for Sanyi! My pains began three days later, at night. I tidied myself up, washed and curled my hair, and we took the first bus to Perechyn, then a train to Uzhhorod. Already on the train the baby wanted very much to come into the world! I was not only suffering from agonizing pain, I was also terrified that it would be born on the train! We managed to get to Uzhhorod, where we jumped into a fourwheeler and were riding to the midwives' training institute at full speed. We arrived there at the last minute; my shoes were snatched off by a nurse while I was being rushed into the delivery room. Öcsi also had the umbilical cord twisted around his neck, but he came into the world without forceps.

After handing me over to the doctor, Sanyi went to his sister's. Although they lived nearby, by the time he got there the telephone message that he had a son had already been waiting for him! And this happened exactly on the ninetieth birthday of his grandfather! The old gentleman did come to visit us in the hospital, although he could barely drag himself up the stairs. He brought me a present, looked at his great-grandson, and asked us to name the baby after him; that was how my son became Imre.

Öcsi and I spent one week in the hospital, then we hurried home to Lia and Nenuka in Turia Bystra. Lia was not at all glad about the baby. We arrived home happily, telling her we had brought a little brother for her. "Take him back!" she demanded. When we put the baby into the cot, Lia jumped in after him with her shoes on: "This is my bed!" When we put the baby into the pram, she cried that it was her pram. She insisted that everything was hers and that the baby should be taken away. She was furious for three days, shouting that she did not want any brother! Then slowly she became interested in bathing the baby, she began admiring his sweet little hands and feet, and eventually she resigned herself to having a younger brother.

My little Lia remained a very bad eater, and we struggled with her a lot. Once she ran away from home. When I found her, she was sitting in the cradle of a Rusyn family and was eating *steranký*! *Steranký* are noodles cut into small pieces, boiled, and eaten with milk. The Rusyns use a swinging cradle, hanging from the ceiling on a rope, which the mother can push or pull from every corner of the room whenever a little rocking is needed. It was this kind of cradle in which Lia was put while she was being fed. Afterwards I also asked Nenuka to make *steranký* for her, but she did not eat it at home. Apparently, she also needed the cradle and the little kids around to give her an appetite.

Rusyn meals were, in general, rather meager because the Rusyns themselves were very poor. They ate what grew up there: potatoes, corn, cabbage, apples. Their main dish was corn porridge. They kept goats for their milk, as well as pigs, which they prepared differently from the way we did. They smoked almost every part of it to take along to work. They also made *strapachký*: potato-noodles with curded sheepcheese, and *steranký*, but my favorite was potatoes baked on embers. The knew how much we loved them, so they often brought us some as a gift. It happened once that we were sent baked potatoes from three different places at the same time. They baked the potatoes until crispy, then put them into a special basket, and shook them until the skin rubbed off completely, and they became an appetizing pink color. They were then put into a nice little basket lined and covered with a napkin.

Unfortunately, my asthma became worse and worse, and the doctors still did not recognize what was wrong with me. My only relief was that Nenuka was so reliable, so much so that I could put my children in her care during my asthmatic bouts. It happened that I spent two full days and nights in an armchair pulled to the open window, covered with blankets, just gasping and choking. Sanyi says sometimes I was barely conscious. My eyes were protruding, and they all believed I was done for. I managed to overcome even the worst bouts, but my general condition did not improve. The disease accompanied me into the nineteen-fifties.

In 1940, we celebrated Christmas with two kids already. It was beautiful. By then Nenuka had learned Hungarian quite well, and I could speak rudimentary Rusyn. We lived in perfect harmony up there in Turia Bystra until 1942.

Sanyi was first called up into the Hungarian army in 1942. At that time he only had to take part in a six-week re-training couse. He was trained to be a cipher officer. The Czechoslovak certificate testifying his officer's rank was accepted, and the Hungarian army took him in at the same rank he reached in the Czech army. The training course took place in Budapest, and since the call-up order was valid for six weeks, he did not have to give up his job. We waited for him patiently. In such periods especially, Nenuka proved to be an invaluable helper. Soon after Sanyi returned home, he was taken for another retraining course; this time from a Czechoslovak teacher into a Hungarian one. By the time we had been over this course, too, the menace of war had already reached us.

CHAPTER 11

In 1942 Sanyi had to join a radio deciphering unit at Oradea (Nagyvárad), now in Romania. He was taken there because he knew Slavic languages. All the eighteen cipher officers in his unit were former Rusyn school teachers. One of them, Ivan, could not speak a word of Hungarian, but he, too, was given the rank of lieutenant. Before going to the front, men with a family were given a three-day leave. Poor Sanyi rushed home to see us. He arrived in Perechyn in the evening, he walked thirty kilometers so that he could be with us at night, then he left at dawn. I accompanied him as far as Uzhhorod.

In October 1942, eight members of Sanyi's radio team were sent to Kiev, while four others were taken right to the river Don (near Stalingrad), where the frontlines had been frozen. The unit sent to the Don was commanded by Sanyi. They had to decipher intercepted Russian telegrams. The addressees of the secret telegrams were denoted by code numbers: telegrams with number 2 were sent for the infantry, those with number 4 were meant for the tanks, while those with number 5 were intended for the air force.

At the curve of the Don, Hungarian soldiers were supposed to hold up the Red Army with guns and light machine-guns—when they did not even have proper winter clothing. Whole lines of soldiers remained frozen on the snow-fields. On January 12, 1943 the Red Army broke through the Hungarian front line, and tens of thousands of men were killed. Sanyi only escaped because the deciphering unit worked behind the front line at the headquarters. Their supplies had also been better there, unlike in the first lines, where the food sometimes had frozen before it reached the soldiers. After the break-through, Sanyi's unit was chased to Kiev, where they also lived through a heavy bombing of the city. Then in September Sanyi was discharged; he had done the one year of service at the front required in the Hungarian Army. He could come home at last!

Sanyi said that the style prevailing in the Hungarian army was very different from what he had been used to in the Czech army. The manner of treatment was rougher, more inhumane. As time passed by and he was promoted to higher and higher ranks, of course, his situation also improved. He was discharged as a lieutenant.

In the spring of 1944, after Sanyi's discharge and before his next call-up, the Jewish inhabitants of Turia Bystra were deported. It shook the whole village, since we all knew one another. Those taken away were respected, popular people: shopkeepers, shoemakers, as well as much-liked pupils of Sanyi. A committee made up of reliable local people took an inventory of the property in the houses left empty so that on their return the owners should find everything without loss. Then the houses were sealed. We do not know what happened to the carefully registered property of the deported. Not one of the owners returned!

Sanyi was called up again in May 1944, this time to a trench mortar battalion. They were trained in Hajdúhadház. Because of a temporary modification of military movements, they were also stationed there for an uncertain time. There was no knowing how long they would stay. They could have been sent to the front at any minute.

Sanyi sent me word that if I wanted to see him, I should go to Hajdúhadház. I did not need to be told twice! I arranged for the children to be looked after. A friend of Nenuka's, who was a nursery school mistress, moved in with her and the two of them took care of the children and the household.

I stood out on the highway and was ready to stop whatever vehicle would come first. A truck came, and the driver offered to take me. He was going to Uzhhorod, but with a long detour by way of Mukachevo. I thought it was better than nothing, so I got in. There were soldiers in the driving compartment, and I expected soldiers to be reliable. I explained to them that I was in such a great hurry because I was visiting my husband, who was going to be taken to the front at any minute. They asked me why I dared to join them, why I was not afraid of them. "I thought a soldier would not harm another soldier's wife, and besides, you look to be so honest," I answered. They said they were honest indeed, but they were partisans, and I would make an excellent cook in their camp! I was afraid I would drop dead the next minute, or would go mad at least! To leave for my husband in the army, and to end up in a partisans' camp, with my two little children waiting for me in

Turia Bystra! When I had turned from pale to green with terror, they took pity on me and told me they were real soldiers, and they recommended that I not hitchhike again, because I could easily be abducted by real partisans.

Eventually I arrived in Uzhhorod safely. I was even able to drop in on Mamuka before the departure of my train to tell her I was going to visit Sanyi. In those months railway traffic was already hard hit by the war, but I managed to get to Hajdúhadház somehow. By the time I got there, Sanyi's battalion had already left.

A friend of mine by the name of Rózsika was there on vacation. Her sister was married to a well-to-do Budapest bank employee, and they had a summer-cottage in Bocskay-kert, a summer resort on the outskirts of Hajdúhadház. I spent four or five days with them. They said Sanyi had often visited them on horseback. He had hoped very much to see me. We barely missed each other! After a few days they put me and Rózsika on a train, saying we should go back to Uzhhorod while it was possible.

At home I found everything in order. Turia Bystra, up in the mountains, would have been protected from the war had the area not been inhabited by partisans! The partisans came to the village at night looting and pillaging. I prepared myself for their visits, but miraculously they always avoided us! They went into every other house, including the houses of other teachers and the parsonage as well. They did not harm the people, but they took everything edible—pigs, chickens— and they emptied the pantries. As I found out later, one of the partisans was a former pupil of Sanyi and liked him very much. He insisted that the teacher's family should be spared during each marauding.

Sanyi and his battalion were sent with their eight trench mortars into northern Romania to stop the advance of the Red Army. He was the commanding officer, while the coordinates were given by telephone from a lieutenant at command headquarters. Sanyi's battalion barely had any ammunition, however! On October 15th, they rejoiced to hear governor Horthy's proclamation ordering an immediate cease-fire. They thought peace had arrived and they could go home. Well, they could not! They did not know anything about the German occupation of Hungary the following day; they just continued the withdrawal. At Battonya, the Soviets had already entered Hungary. At Satu Mare (Hungarian: Szatmárnémeti), about 75 kilometers southeast of Uzhhorod, the Hungarians were still holding their positions, although Nyíregyháza about

100 kilometers west of Satu Mare was already occupied by the Soviets. While withdrawing, Sanyi's unit also had to fight their way through the Nyíregyháza sector of the front line. At home in Turia Bystra, my coughing bouts were becoming more and more frequent, and they were also accompanied by spasms of abdominal pain. Just when the situation became unbearable, my Sanyi turned up; he had received a few days' leave. He immediately took us to Uzhhorod, put the children up with Mamuka, and took me to the hospital, where I was immediately operated on for appendicitis. Sanyi returned to Turia Bystra together with Mamuka, who was to remain there to take care of the children while I was in the hospital. This proved to be a very good decision, because when they arrived home, a dispatch ordering Sanyi to interrupt his leave and to return to his battalion right away had been waiting for him. Sanyi explained our situation to his commanders, who extended his leave for a few days. So after a successful operation Sanyi himself took me home from the hospital. He put me in the care of Mamuka, and hurried back to his command. We did not see each other again until the end of the war. I only received laconic army postcards: "I am all right; take care of yourselves!" We also sent similar cards to him.

Late in fall, in November, Sanyi's battalion advanced to attack at Füzesabony. It was raining so heavily that they could only fire if projectiles were rolled into gunpowder which gave them an extra jerk. By the time they finished rolling, there was nothing to shoot at because the enemy had already moved on. When they were done with trenching their eight mortars and directing them on the target, they noticed that the German soldiers were fleeing! It was raining so heavily that they could barely orient themselves. The others took shelter in a house; Sanyi was the only one to remain outside. All of a sudden, he realized there were people behind him. He looked back and saw about thirty Russian soldiers approaching.

They were very much surprised when he said good morning to them in Russian. They made him throw away his weapon and call out his comrades from the house. The latter also laid down their arms, then lined up. They were taken under armed escort to a Soviet colonel, who asked Sanyi where he had learned Russian so well. He explained that he was from Subcarpathia, and on inquiry he also added he was a schoolteacher by training. The colonel came to like Sanyi, and wanted him to become his interpreter. Sanyi could choose between two alternatives:

going with them as their interpreter, and then returning home to Uzhhorod, or becoming a prisoner of war, and being taken with the other POWs to a camp. He chose to go with them, but he was not a soldier of the Red Army for a minute. He was allowed to wear his Hungarian uniform; he only had to remove his insignia of lieutenancy. He was very lucky with that colonel! A friend of his, Rezső Steingruber, was taken to a POW camp in Bodajbo, about two thousand kilometers east of Lake Baikal, and was kept there for ten years!

In the fall of 1944, when Sanyi was taken captive, we got a telegram from the Laszota family in Uzhhorod, saying: "Come immediately!" At that time I was looking after four children. A friend of mine and a colleague of Sanyi's from Turia Bystra, Boriska, had to be taken to the Uzhhorod hospital for an ectopic pregnancy. Her husband was also in the army, but at one point he received a few days' leave; it was that leave which resulted in her ill-fated pregnancy. When Boriska was taken away in the ambulance, she left her two children in my care. After receiving the telegram, I hired a villager with a cart and packed up the four children. We could already hear the Soviet rocket-throwers called *katyushas* barking in the distance. We could see missiles called "Stalin's candles" flying about, and there were also bombardments. Turia Bystra was not being bombarded, but the acetone factory and railway station in nearby Perechyn were. It was imprudent to leave in those conditions, but I was afraid of what might lie ahead for us. We were two young women with four small children. Our side was about to lose the war, and woe to the vanquished! Our future seemed safer in Uzhhorod with the larger family. I suppose that was why they also thought to send us the telegram.

I laid our couch across the cart, and I filled the hollow inside it with bedclothes, food, bottles of jam, which all broke on the way, and our stock of milk, which was shaken into butter. I put the four kids on the couch, and I sat next to the driver. Eighteen kilometers from Uzhhorod we were caught in heavy bombing. The horses bolted, and ran away with the cart. We jumped off the driver's seat, and the driver snatched off two children from the left, while I whipped off the other two from the right. The horses galloped right into the stream, where the cart turned over. We did not know where to run, bombs were dropping ahead us, behind us, everywhere! Fortunately, our driver was a nice, quiet, helpful man. He picked up two kids and started running toward a house which provided some shelter. I followed him with the two other kids.

After we had been put in relative safety, the driver went back to the stream to unharness and calm down the horses. Then he sought help so that he could set the cart upright and pull it out of the stream. I had experienced utmost terror, the worst in my life! Then it was all over; perfect silence overtook us. We put the cart and its "load" into order as much as we could, and we set out again. On the way we survived another bombing, but this time it did not startle the horses. We waited until the end of the air-raid in the courtyard of an abandoned house. We arrived at my parents-in-law's late in the evening, battered but in one piece. My father-in-law had already been very anxious because he expected us early in the afternoon.

Meantime, the room which was at our disposal in Mamuka's house had been occupied by the army. So after a day like that we still could not have a rest. We had to go on to my sister-in-law's place. They did not live far, but both the children and I were already worn out.

Whereas Mamuka's rooms were taken by Hungarian and German soldiers, my sister-in-law's house was occupied by tenants, so we could only find a small empty room in the courtyard. We unloaded our belongings, and I put the children to bed at last. Then I notified the relatives of my friend Boriska that her two children were with me, and the relatives came to fetch them. They learned from me that Boriska had been in the hospital.

The small room in my sister-in-law's house was not suitable for a longer stay. Therefore, the next day I set out to look for an apartment for us, but in vain. By that time the Uzhhorod Jews had been deported. Their apartments were empty, and one could apply to the local government to be temporarily put up in one of them. After all my attempts to find an apartment had failed, I found no other solution but to apply. I was assigned the apartment of a former friend of mine, Ibolya Katz, in the courtyard of Aunt Olga. The Katzs were all deported by the Germans, and none of them survived the Holocaust. We had earnestly conspired to save Ibolya, but we failed.

We started life in Uzhhorod with a few pieces of furniture belonging to the Katzs, my couch brought from Turia Bystra, and a table and some chairs presented to us by friends. Although my sister-in-law was not very interested in how we were, the people around us, Aunt Olga and Aunt Annus Klein who lived next door, cared about us.

Aunt Annus Klein had not been deported, unlike her husband. Uncle Béla Klein had been hiding with my parents-in-law, until a friend of

Aunt Annus's ran over to him with the news that the horror was over and he could safely go home. He did, and he enjoyed the company of his family for a while, but then, because of a broken pipe, he ran for a plumber. He was captured in the street, and he was deported and killed. Had he stayed in hiding just a day longer, he would ahve survived. When Aunt Annus's friend ran for him, the Soviets were merely reported to be close, but by the following day they had marched in. Aunt Annus was a Christian woman, and Uncle Béla had also become Christian when they got married. So their daughter, Edit, was naturally also born a Christian. This fact helped at first: when Uncle Béla and Edit were taken to the ghetto, they could still get out again upon presenting their certificates of baptism. Afterwards, however, only the lineage mattered, and Uncle Béla disappeared for good. Edit survived, and later she and Aunt Annus emigrated to Israel. It was in Israel that Aunt Annus died.

The families forced into the ghetto and those outside were first strictly forbidden to communicate with each other. Later the rigor was somewhat relaxed. The guards turned away when friends or acquaintances brought food to the fence of the ghetto. A friend of mine originally from Uzhhorod, Kati Bán, who is now a pediatrician in Budapest, told me that each time she visits Uzhhorod she goes to see Ica, a former classmate of hers, whom her mother sent to the ghetto with a basket packed with food every day. She thought that the guards would perhaps be more lenient with children, and she was right. That was how Kati's family managed warm meals.

The German occupation of Uzhhorod was short, but all the more dreadful. There was not a single person in the city who welcomed it. Most people dreaded just the same the Soviet, or as they called it, "Russian" occupation, but there were also people who looked forward to it. There were already a few Communists in Uzhhorod, and they expected that the Soviet occupation would open up new possibilities for them in the new era. For the persecuted, the Soviets really meant liberation and rescue, at least, for a while.

A few days before the Soviets marched in, Aunt Olga and her daughter Rózsika managed to get to Budapest to visit Aunt Olga's elder daughter. Their large apartment that faced the street had a single inhabitant left: Uncle János, Aunt Olga's husband. The apartments facing the courtyard had had Jewish tenants, who had all been deported; only my two children and I stayed there. The whole huge, two-storey complex of apartments was inhabited by four of us: Uncle János, the two children, and I. Well, the silence that we experienced after the departure of Aunt Olga and Rózsika did not last long. The Soviets came in, and in a minute, every room, every closet became full of soldiers. They also put themselves up with lonely women and children. They were rude and dirty. They were frightening! Uncle János offered to put us up in his apartment. He thought it would be safer for us there, and perhaps we could also cope with the difficulties better together.

We hoped this situation would not last long, and we could go on living in a Subcarpathia belonging to Hungary. Of course, those who thought about the future seriously, without illusions, soon left. More and more people were escaping to the West. The luckier found their way right away. Others landed in camps, and had to stay there until their relatives or acquaintances sent them official invitations.

Returning to our everyday problems: when we left Turia Bystra by cart, my pig and chickens remained home. My pig was a charming animal; it had a nice pink color and a turned-up nose. Whenever I sat down with the kids in the garden, it came up to us fawning and lay down near us expecting to be scratched below his ears. Nenuka and I raised our pet into a large, beautiful animal. Just before the Soviet occupation, I ran up to Turia Bystra and had the pig slaughtered and prepared. I brought the various kinds of delicacies made from it down to Uzhhorod, so for a long time we had something to depend on. Of course we shared it with the others, first and foremost with Aunt Annus, Edit, and Uncle János.

There were frequent air-raid warnings because the bridges were heavily bombed. Eventually all three bridges in Uzhhorod were destroyed. Fortunately, the house had a cellar which opened from inside the house. Uncle János used to work in peace time as a plumber, and the cellar served as his workshop and storage room. We spent most of the time down there. One of its rooms was a bedroom for the kids, and the adults used the other one as a sitting room.

Öcsi became seriously ill and had a very high fever. Everybody tried to help him. They gave him whatever delicacy was still left in their households. We managed to find some sugar and lemon, so we tried to cure him with tea, a little soup, and with cold compresses. There was not much we could really do, and the child became fainter and fainter. When it was quiet outside, I took him up for fresh air. It took Öcsi a long time to overcome the disease. In this period, when we went

from one terrifying situation into the other, the childen became insepa-
rable from me. They went through the war practically stuck to my body.

Nenuka undertook to preserve our home in Turia Bystra, supported
by her friend and by our puli dog "Bleki." It was not her fault that she
did not succeed. Villagers robbed us of all our belongings. Turia Bystra,
too, had its stratum of those with no respect for person, time or place,
no respect for God or man. Those people took advantage of the wartime chaos. My hens, ducks, and geese were also stolen. I was lucky to
have saved our pig in time. At one point I hired a truck to fetch our
belongings, but I found only a few items in the house: some books and
small personal belongings of no value to the thieves. I arrived back in
Uzhhorod with an empty truck. We had nothing left, except the few
pieces of clothing that I had thrown into the container of my couch
when we fled by cart.

In addition to our furniture, our linen, our dinner-sets and other
household items, we were robbed of all our clothes. We had once had
full wardrobes: nice, fashionable, quality clothes for all seasons. I had
always set a high value on beautiful clothes, and had always found
pleasure in taking care of them. In those times, a teacher and his family
were, in fact, expected to be well-dressed. Sanyi had an elegant black
suit, as well as a brown and a grey one, and then a lighter grey suit, a
summer suit, and naturally a dinner-jacket. He had had his dinner-jacket
made for our wedding, and since luckily he kept his figure, he could
wear it for a long time. My wonderful American evening dress, the one
in which I had such a great success in the first-class lounge of the ocean-
liner, had been monopolized by my sister-in-law. Her niece, who could
draw excellently, even made a portrait of her in my evening dress! My
sister-in-law decided I did not need an evening dress in Turia Bystra. It
was true, but I could very well have used the basic dress as a nightgown. I have always considered beautiful underwear more important
than outwardly beautiful dresses. I found the greatest pleasure in wearing something beautiful that nobody could see, except maybe Sanyi. I
insisted on wearing beautiful underwear also in the greatest poverty,
and I have always managed somehow. God is good!

The house of Aunt Annus Klein became the center of our circle of
friends. Uncle Béla had been a respected clerk for the electricity works.
Aunt Annus and Edit were also popular and regarded highly by everybody. When the Germans left, the young Jewish men in hiding came
forward and they also ended up in the house of the Klein family. It was

then that we found out how many of them managed to hide. They helped me to move my belongings over the fence, because eventually I was also taken in by Aunt Annus.

The children slept with Aunt Annus in Uncle Béla's bed, whereas I shared a room with Editke. The younger sister of Aunt Annus lived in the third room, while two further rooms were occupied by Russian officers. These two officers fortunately proved to be pleasant people. Seeing the difficult conditions we lived in, they sometimes brought us a little sugar; at another occasion, a goose.

My mother-in-law and my sister-in-law did not have much space in their houses, but to tell the truth they did not much care about us, either. Shopowners were thriving in those days, and, accordingly, they also had a very active social life. Amidst their many different kinds of occupation, my sister-in-law and her husband forgot about us! It was only my father-in-law who was interested in how we were doing. He faithfully visited us in Aunt Annus's house.

It was time to look for some means of subsistence. The remains of my pig did not last long, because many of us depended on them. I did not want to live off Aunt Annus. The interests of the dollar loan were paid to me neither in dollars nor in food. My sister-in-law calculated before the great inflation how much they were worth in Hungarian pengôs, and then she stuck to the *pengő* and to the rate she calculated even when the *pengő* was not worth anything anymore. Incidentally, there were three kinds of money in use simultaneously: the Czech crown, the Hungarian *pengő*, and the Soviet *chervontsi*.

My sister-in-law and her husband, Cirill Fundanics, were about to get a divorce. The ground of divorce was András, my next brother-in-law. Allegedly he was a former great love of my sister-in-law, but nobody knew about him. Neither did we know that her husband Cirill also cheated on her from time to time. We came to like András very much: he had a first-class brain, an exceptionally good heart, and he was a gentleman from head to toe. In the Hungarian era, András had a good position in the center of a nation-wide network of consumers' cooperatives in Budapest. He studied commercial management there. Then he came home to Uzhhorod. His wife had stayed on in Budapest for some time. When she followed András, it was already too late, and they were soon divorced.

CHAPTER 12

At the end of the war, after the Soviet occupation, András was commissioned to revive commerce in Uzhhorod and to restart and expand a network of shops operated before by a consumers' cooperative. Two young Jewish men and I were put in charge of the first store, a toyshop. András collected all the toys available in Uzhhorod and left to us everything else from pricing to selling. This shop became my first work place, and I worked there as a cashier. In a month we sold out of everything. The cooperative opened more and more shops. After a while, it also established food stores, which sold the contents of American UNRRA [United Nations Relief and Rehabilitation Administration] packages for food coupons. I was very lucky with those American packages. People had an aversion to peanut butter, because it was unknown to them. They did not know what to do with it. Since nobody wanted peanut butter, I could take home large boxes of it and at last I had something to spread on my children's bread. It warmed my heart, too: it tasted like home.

In January 1945 we reopened a porcelain crystal shop which had been sealed when its owner was deported, and we sold its stock of goods. I was a cashier in that shop as well. One after the other the stock of all the sealed shops whose owners had been deported or were absent was sold off.

Commerce was expanding every day. András, the managing director of the cooperative, created with amazing skills a whole network of shops selling all kinds of goods. New shops were opened where others had been emptied. András soon gave me the cashier's job in a newly established central office that controlled the food shops. The incomes of all the grocer's, butcher's, bakeries, and restaurants collected in my hands—unfortunately only after closing time every day. The real difficulty consisted in the fact that the income came to me in three different kinds of money which had to be counted and entered into the books separately. In the end I had to make the balance in *chervontsi*—and what is more, in Russian. And that was a time when I could not even spell my name in Cyrillic letters. It was Jóska, the general factotum of our office, who taught me to spell in Russian the numbers, my name, the names of our company and the shops belonging to it, and the name of the bank. I learned the most important things within one week. Every day when I finished with the balance, I still had to carry the three bags of money, with huge amounts in each, to the bank and wait until they were counted. I was glad to have work, but it was awful to arrive home late at night completely worn out day after day.

I worked diligently. My work was very hard, and I did not earn more than a cleaner would have, but it was worth it because it ensured me good "procurement" opportunities. In those days procurement was the central and most difficult task of every family. Everything from bread to soap was rationed and could be obtained for a coupon, provided the given commodity was available. Coupons were distributed by the housing-estate managements, and people were entitled to them by right of citizenship. If the commodity you wanted for your coupon was available, you still had to stand in a queue for half a day to get it, and you also needed to be lucky that they not run out before your turn came. Since I worked at the center of a network of shops, I could get everything I needed. We always got our rations of bread and meat. What was more, I received choice goods for our coupons and, when it was possible, also for the coupons of our neighbors. When a consignment of sugar arrived, the manager of almost every shop brought us some as a present. Despite the rationing, they were able to save a little. In those days lump sugar was sold in bars, and shop managers surprised each office clerk with a bar. We (including my parents-in-law) had bread coupons for five persons. If I bought bread for each, and especially if I also got some bread as a present from the bakery managers, we even had some leftover which my father-in-law could sell in the street. The little money he earned I spent on a little butter for our bread. That was how we lived; working a lot, and finessing and maneuvering constantly.

The commanding officer for the city ordered everything to be taken into state property immediately. Whether one resisted or not, everything was taken away. The land, tractors, horses, carts, shops, workshops, everything was expropriated. Those who had eight to ten acres of land were not only robbed of their land but were also declared to be kulaks or "rich peasants," and were sent to Siberia. The former owners were not allowed to pursue their trade as employees either because they were regarded as "bourgeois profiteers." Everyone was given a job other than what he was qualified for. Cirill Fundánics, my former brother-in-law, who had owned a shop and was every inch a merchant, was given a job as a joiner in a plywood factory.

My father-in-law's workshop was also expropriated, but he was at least allowed to work in his own profession: he had to look after the harnesses in a collective farm. He, who had always been independent, became an employee in his old age. His death was also caused by a cold he caught at the collective farm. My parents-in-law's apartment house, which they had inherited from their parents, was taken away somewhat later, but for a while at least it helped their survival even though it was so heavily taxed that hardly anything was left from the rents they collected.

Gyula Prokop, the son of Sanyi's godfather, had a thriving independent butcher's shop and did not intend to give it up. When he was first hit with an extraordinary tax of 90,000 *pengő*, he paid it. He paid it the second time, too. The third time he hanged himself.

During the war I had no contact with my American family. Mommy had some news about us, though. She knew what a difficult situation we were in because she kept in touch with Gizike, the daughter of Aunt Olga living in Budapest. We were only able to resume contact after more than six years had passed. I received the first letter from America in 1949, and from that time on we were allowed to correspond under the careful supervision of the authorities.

Slowly the English language also disappeared from my life. At first I still had English books, but later there were no books left, and neither were any conversation partners available. I had to adapt myself. I had to learn Rusyn. Rusyn is different both from Ukrainian and from Russian, although these three languages are mutually intelligible. I can use all three, but I have not learned the standard literary version of any of them. Neither have I learned literary Hungarian. English was the only langauge that I could speak impeccably, instinctively, and consciously at the same time, but I have not used it for sixty years. There was an exception, though!

In the winter of 1944 Edit Klein discovered a group of young cyclists on the Uzhhorod promenade. She had learned some English, so she could tell that they were speaking in English. She ran home and called me to talk to them and to find out where they had come from.

Well, they were young men from the United States on a bicycle tour—
in the middle of the war, in December! I told them I had come from
New Jersey a few years before, and I asked them if perhaps they were
from New Jersey, too. I would have liked to have gotten some information about my family and my acquaintances, but, unfortunately, they
were all from North Dakota. We had a brief, friendly conversation. We
did not even hint at politics. It gave me pleasure to talk to my compatri-
ots after so many years, and we went home in a good mood.

Late at night, after I had put the children to bed, and I myself had
already washed but still sat up barefoot for a while talking with the
other adults, there was a knock at the door. Some men wanted to check
our identity papers. I identified myself with my American passport. On
the one hand, that was the only ID I had, and on the other hand, I was
also proud of it; I showed it off as a conscientious American citizen.
Besides, I knew America and the Soviets were allies! Despite the alliance I was ordered to go with the men, because the document I presented was unknown to them. I wanted to put on my stockings and my
coat, but they said it was unnecessary; it was warm in the car, and
besides, they would only take me for five minutes until my passport
was checked. Well, they drove around Uzhhorod at least ten times so
that I could not identify where I was taken. Eventually I found myself
at the headquarters of the secret police, called Bezpeka in Ukrainian,
and I suspected that I had been arrested.

I was interrogated the entire night. I had to put down in writing
what had happened between the cyclists and me, and how it had happened. I had nothing to hide, so I sincerely related my innocent encounter with the American team and then put it down in writing, too.
Naturally, I could only write in English and Hungarian. Then I was left
alone with a guard and I had to wait. At four a.m. another man started
interrogating me, to whom I had to relate and describe again what I had
already related and described several times. I had to endure this for
three days, with no stockings and no proper clothing on. I was given
some food, but it did not go down my throat.

On the third day during my usual evening interrogation I was told
that I could go home. What was more, they packed up some oranges,
lemons, cans of food, tea, and coffee for me to take home. I was both
amazed and suspicious. I had no idea what was going on. On the second day of my detention, during my interrogation I overheard the voice
of a Jewish friend of mine: Karcsi. I found out only later that Karcsi

was there to intercede on my behalf. He was known and trusted by my interrogators, and he managed to convince them that I had nothing to do with either spying or politics.

I could leave for home, at last, in my three-day-old underwear and house-dress, without stockings and without an overcoat in the sub-zero December cold. I was overwhelmed by fear and uncertainty. I looked behind me every minute. I was sure I was being followed. I checked in the beautiful large shop-windows of the promenade to see if there was someone behind me. At last I got home. I could not say a word. I was shaking and sobbing. The others were also crying. They had no idea where I had been taken, let alone why. They were only told I was under arrest. I put down the package and sank into a chair, shivering with cold and fear. It was Christmas, the Christmas of 1944.

The young Jewish friends of Aunt Annus prepared a wonderful Christmas for us. They gathered all their childhood toys that they could find, and they even got a Christmas tree from somewhere. The delicacies of the package from the Bezpeka also added to the luster of the holiday.

As I said before, at that time procurement was the main concern of every family. We were less affected by this problem, but our lives also centered around selling, buying, tracking down, obtaining, and standing in line. As long as people had something to sell, their misery was alleviated by the Thursday fairs. We also sold every item of our furniture and wardrobe that seemed dispensable. The new settlers, the well-off Russian soldiers and their wives, bought up everything. It happened that a Russian "young lady" came across me in the street in my nightgown. She bought it from me at a Thursday fair and wore it as her Sunday best. In our miserable, defenceless situation we enjoyed laughing at the awfully boorish wives of the new masters.

The families of Russian soldiers immediately occupied the empty apartments of the deported Jewish families. Many of those Jews who survived the Holocaust emigrated to Israel, America, or Australia right away, and their apartments were also taken by Russians. From our circle of friends almost no one returned. After Edit Klein ascertained that there was no hope of her father returning, she moved with her mother and husband to a territory under Czechoslovak sovereignty, and at the end of the fifties they moved on to Israel.

The story of Joli, one of Mamuka's tenants, has a happy ending. She managed to come home from a concentration camp and then married an elderly widower, a tailor by profession. The tailor's grown-up sons from his first marriage were running a large clothing factory in America. The quality of the parcels sent by them indicated that they lived in very good conditions in the United States. Jolika and her husband had two daughters, and they led a harmonious family life. The American sons accepted their father's new family and invited them to the States. They applied for an emigration permit many times. By the time they got it, the tailor had died, and their elder daughter had married an Uzhhorod man of Armenian descent. Jolika however emigrated with her younger daughter, and they started a new life with the help of her stepsons. She started working in their clothing factory, and they moved into a house of their own. Two years later her elder daughter and her Armenian son-in-law also followed them.

Returning to our new masters: many of the Soviet soldiers occupying the city were left behind in Uzhhorod for good to run the new local government. They carried out great destruction in the apartments where they were put up, so that everybody was glad when barracks were set up for them. They moved to the barracks from the private apartments in the summer of 1945, but during the winter of 1944-45 we still had them as our "guests."

After my arrest at Christmas, 1944, my parents-in-law suddenly realized that my children and I shouldn't be staying with non-family in such hard times after all, and they took the children with them. I still remained with the Kleins for a while because my parents-in-law's house was farther away from the center and I was afraid to go home by myself from the bank late at night. The downtown apartment of Aunt Annus could be reached faster and by a safer route.

After a while the crown and the *pengő* ceased to exist; only the *chervontsi* remained in use. This made my work considerably simpler, but those who had savings in crowns or *pengő* lost everything they had. In our family, too, our *pengő* became but toys for children.

In the meantime Sanyi advanced with the Soviet colonel as far as Prague. He was not needed anymore after Prague, so on May 9, 1945 he was set free with proper documents. The colonel first handed over Sanyi as a POW to his headquarters, but then immediately arranged for him to be released. The colonel even took him to the railway station and put him on a troop train going across Uzhhorod. It took Sanyi three days to get home. On the way he got off at Leles, because he did not exclude the possibility that we might be staying there with my relatives. Since he found none of us at Lelesz he went on, and on May 13, 1945, on a beautiful warm summer night he arrived home.

God is gracious: Sanyi managed to endure everything, and we also stuck it out! We were alive, and we were together again!

CHAPTER 13

Subcarpathia was divided into three zones, depending on the distance from the borders. We belonged to zone two. The border between zones could only be crossed with a permit. For example, if I wanted to go to the neighboring town of Chop, in zone one, I had to obtain permission. Zone three extended over the Carpathians. It was totally impossible to travel to Moscow. Prague was our only gate to the world, since the border to Prague was not yet completely sealed off. Clever people regularly went to Prague on "procurement trips," to buy and sell, or to barter.

I became sicker and sicker. My asthma kept tormenting me, and I also had heart problems. I decided I would go to Prague and try to arrange our emigration to America. András, my brother-in-law, found it an excellent idea and recommended a truck bound for Prague. His cooperative had close connections with Prague since they exchanged goods. András gave me an official document according to which I, an employee of the cooperative, was accompanying the truck in the capacity of a driver's mate. I travelled on the platform of the truck all the way from Uzhhorod to Prague. Fortunately, we had a warm summer. Because of the platform's position I did not see much of the scenery. I mostly slept or talked with the other seven "driver's mates." We had a good journey to Prague. Our truck was not stopped even once.

In Prague I looked for the embassy of the United States and I put forth my request. They did not promise me anything. They said my husband was an officer in a hostile army. "What officer in what army?" I asked. Sanyi had been discharged much earlier, not only as a Hungarian officer but also as a POW, and Uzhhorod had been occupied by the Soviets for good. My husband was neither an officer nor hostile. I found it unbelievable that Sanyi should be seen as a threat to the United States. At that time Sanyi was already willing to emigrate. The Soviet officers whom he interpreted for and made friends with knew already what was ahead for us. They had bitter first-hand experience of the nature of the Soviet Union. They urged Sanyi to go to the West, the farther the better, as long as it was possible. We did not quite understand why honest, hard-working people, who did not go in for politics or for crime, should escape leaving their homes behind. Sanyi's Russian friends only answered that they wished we would never get to know why. "Go before it is too late!" they kept repeating. They had convinced us, but in vain. My home country did not want all four of us, and I did not have the slightest intention of going back without Sanyi. I left Prague without having achieved anything.

On the way back there were fewer of us on the platform. Most people were heading for the West. There were two women besides me, and Dezső Zádor, an Uzhhorod composer, who joined us in Prague. When the truck was about to leave for home, an unknown man asked the driver if he could join us. We had plenty of room, so we took him; it was natural in those days. We were already near the new Slovak-Soviet border when he pulled out a weapon and hijacked the truck. We did not know if he was a partisan or just a criminal. He made us drive on unknown roads to an unknown destination. At one point the man ordered the driver to stop and he got out. Our driver, who also had a weapon but so far was not in a position to use it, pulled out his weapon and shot the man as he was walking away. The stranger dropped dead.

The police arrived soon to investigate the matter. We were all taken to Košice in eastern Slovakia and put into prison. We spent two days in the Košice jailhouse while everybody was interrogated several times. Our truck was parked in the courtyard of the police the entire time. Despite this fact, everything movable had been stolen from the truck by the time we were set free. This time I had to leave literally empty-handed. In addition to not settling anything, I was robbed of my handbag with all my personal belongings, including the little presents I had bought for my children. That was how my first attempt to get back to America ended.

CHAPTER 14

S anyi's nerves were not really fit for teaching any longer. Furthermore, well-informed acquaintances warned us that in the new system teachers were made to bear all kinds of tasks besides teaching, what was more, mainly political tasks. It was teachers who had to organize political meetings, the elections of representatives, and the innumerable "battles" of the "ideological warfare." It was obvious that in the new era, being a teacher would be incompatible with having a clear conscience. So Sanyi chose not to teach again. Once he was called upon to resume teaching, but at that time he had already been working in commerce, and he was allowed to stay.

Sanyi found a job with the help of András, our brother-in- law, in the new state-controlled consumers' cooperative which was established in place of the local unit of a prewar system of consumers' cooperatives. He had to organize a network of village shops, tea rooms and snackbars. There was no private capital, there were no private merchants, and there were practically no people left with the proper qualifications. Sanyi and his colleagues had to build up the whole network out of nothing, and they managed to do it. Afterwards Sanyi worked as a kind of accountant. His job was to determine prices for the products sold in the network's shops. He could have made a greater career for himself if he had been willing to render services of another kind as well, but he always refused to do so.

We had to settle for a new life. We could not expect help from Sanyi's parents indefinitely. They were also hit hard by the new system. Their savings had come to nothing, and they barely had any income. My father-in-law repaired the harnesses of a collective farm for almost nothing. At first they still received a small amount from the rents of a house they owned in Munkácsi Street, but after the death of my father-in-law that house was also expropriated, which left Mamuka without any income whatsoever.

My parents-in-law could keep their own house on Kapos Street, and we partitioned a room off in their house, and had a separate entrance and a kitchen built for it. That was how we established an independent home for our family. The furniture was brought together by friends. Some gave us a chair, others a wardrobe or a bed. All in all, our room was quite nicely furnished eventually. We had two beds, one of which was shared by the children, the other—a couch which could be opened into a double bed—Sanyi and I shared. Each of the four chairs that we had were different because we received each one from a different person. Bedding was given to us by my mother-in-law, but my sister-in-law also contributed to our household with two eiderdown pillows. We obtained a radio in 1952 when a family we knew well were granted permission to emigrate to Hungary, and before moving they sold us their Soviet-made portable radio.

We had a wooden floor which I waxed and polished, so as not to have to scrub it with lyed water. It was more convenient for me that way. I covered the floor with handwoven carpets. First we heated the house with an iron stove, then I had a tile stove made which burned both wood and coal. Through my work place we could obtain cheap wood, which we supplemented with quality coal from Silesia. So my Sanyi had ample opportunity again to indulge in wood-splitting. Our kitchen was heated with the cooking range. It was many, many years later that we obtained a gas cooker attached to a gas balloon.

Such a small apartment is bearable only if it is kept in order; if everything is always put in its place. Even our children learned this very quickly. Our only wardrobe provided more than enough room for all our clothes. Our shoes and other, less delicate belongings were kept in a container under the children's bed. The bedding was piled up and covered with a nice blanket on our bed. Despite the dire circumstances our home was never messy. We were ready to receive visitors at any time.

I had never been close to my mother-in-law, but we had never quarrelled either. Although we shared a house, we led independent lives, had different ways of living, and also kept our households strictly apart. Both of us preferred it that way. In fact, she was a reliable, careful grandmother, and she did look after her grandchildren, but she did not show any tenderness or devotion.

The children first attended a nursery school run by nuns. At that time nuns still existed, but they were soon dispersed; all sisterhoods and brotherhoods were abolished. Lia started school in the fall of 1945.

We could only choose between Russian and Ukrainian schools—in a Hungarian city! But at least the school was not far. The kids only had to go to the end of our street. At first I accompanied them to school, but they objected to it. Then I followed them in secret for a while, but I had to admit to myself it was unnecessary. There were no cars in the city; at best a four-wheeler or a cart appeared in the streets on occasion.

In the mornings I dressed Lia in the obligatory brown uniform with a black apron. I did not adopt the Russian habit of huge bows; I simply braided Lia's hair. The horrible-looking and unmanageable uniform also had to be worn on holidays, but then with a white apron. We tried to make at least the little white apron look pretty. We sewed it from a fine batist, and starched and ironed it carefully. I ironed the ugly brown dress every day, but the pleats didn't last long, unlike the creases. The boys' uniform was even uglier—a brown shirt with a stand-up collar and dark trousers. I never actually bought this horrible outfit for Öcsi. Since I always dressed him in dark clothes anyway, we got away with it. As for girls, on the other hand, there was no excuse, no mercy; the uniform had to be worn.

I had only two cotton dresses left. I kept alternating, washing, and ironing those two dresses continually. In the mornings, after getting up and preparing breakfast, my main concern was ironing. Our income was so small that there was absolutely no money left for clothing. In the winter I wore a jacket of my husband's instead of a winter coat. We could begin to care about what we wore only several years later, when we were allowed to receive parcels from America. My winter coat problem could not wait so long! Edit Klein had a friend who, having lost her fashion studio, took up sewing in her home. She gave me some work: I would finish the dresses she made. She paid me back with a beautiful winter coat instead of money, which was an ideal solution for both of us.

Later it was no longer impossible to buy quality materials, and it was affordable to have a dress made. There were home-made fashions, too. Skillful women with rich imaginations designed lovely dresses and then stitched the designs for the seamstresses.

My children did have a few pieces of clothing left, and if they needed something I always managed somehow to scrape together the money for it. Little Lia, for example, got a cute rabbit-skin coat for winter.

After a few years a Hungarian school opened in Uzhhorod! Most Hungarian parents were absolutely thrilled that their children could learn in their mother tongue, and transferred them to the new school. I was happy as a lark, too. Sanyi's family, however, were of a different opinion. They thought children must study in the official language of the state. "Serious people think of the future, and our future is a Soviet future," they argued. They did not believe the Soviet sovereignty over Subcarpathia was transitory. I got into a fierce fight with the family, and it was the first time I stood up for myself. "So far you have interfered in everything," I said. "Concerning the schooling of my children I accept no advice." I had nothing left in the world but my two children. I decided not to tolerate any interference in their education. Nevertheless, the family did not give up. They tried to persuade me every year to transfer the children to a Russian school. My son actually had some difficulties in the first year of the university, where he had to study in Russian, but he pulled through. There was no other disadvantage to the Hungarian school. It was worth it! A mother does indeed sense what is best for her children!

True, by that time everything went on in Russian, and one could make a career only in Russian. Part of the population was also responsible for that situation. The only Russians in the city were those families who had been settled there to run the administration. However, many non-Russians also declared themselves to be Russians, hoping for better opportunities. The citizens of Uzhhorod resorted to desperate measures in trying to get by. As a consequence, the official statistics soon indicated a Russian majority in the city.

Our subsistence was facilitated by our large yard. We had two walnut trees, five plum trees, an apple tree, a cherry tree, and, of course, a vegetable garden. The yard also included a large grass plot. That was the place where we lived and played with the children in good weather. We kept a ping-pong table there, among other things. Our orchard was connected to the yards of our neighbors. We also had a little courtyard only for ourselves, where we built parallel bars and other kinds of gymnastic apparatus for Lia.

Although Lia had dolls, she preferred to play outside or to do physical excercises. Both Lia and Öcsi were strong, healthy, cheerful kids, excellent gymnasts and good swimmers. They had very good company; they belonged to a group of nice little kids from our neighborhood. When the Tarzan films were on, they all played "Tarzan" in the willow trees. At other times they played indians or soldiers in the large, connecting gardens. Their gang had an island in the river Uzh, which they could reach almost dry-footed on a path known only to them.

One of their adventures involving their island in the Uzh frightened and upset me so much that I could not refrain from spanking them, although I never, ever lifted my hand against them otherwise. One day I could not find my children anywhere. It was late in the evening, and they were still out of sight. First I looked for them in their grandparents' home, but they were not there. Then I ran to our neighbors'. It turned out that all the children from our street were missing, what was more, all the children from the next street as well. The desperate parents formed groups and started to look for them in every possible direction. All of a sudden, they darted out from somewhere with a deafening yell the way they saw it in the war movies. "Hurraaaaaah" (more precisely: *Gurraaaaah* in the Russian way), we won!" shouted the Kapos Street gang. The Bárdos Street gang rushed out from another direction with the same "Hurrah, we won" yell. Their eyes were shining with pride, pleasure, and satisfaction. It was a crisp fall night, and their clothes were dripping with water. Because of the fright caused by their disappearance and because of the icy water I lost my temper and spanked them. When I saw them afterwards sitting on the fence and counting the prints of my fingers on their skin, I already regretted it very much!

They told us that the two gangs of children from two neighboring streets had been preparing for a battle for months. They were on very good terms with each other, so it was not a showdown between them! They saw lots of war movies, in fact, they saw nothing but war movies, and they decided they would play real war. The boys had been carving weapons for months, while the girls prepared to be medical orderlies. They compiled a doctor's bag, bandages, and surgical instruments. Our dexterous Lia was assigned to prepare, by drawing, cutting, and glueing, the medals. Naturally the two gangs became the two parties fighting each other, and their island in the Uzh was selected as the battle site. The "historic" day came at last! The two armies lined up on either side of the Uzh, and invaded the island from both directions. The ice-cold water did not cool their ardour in the least. The boys were entirely absorbed in fencing and they had a great time. The poor girls were waiting for the wounded in vain, even though they were very well prepared. Their time came when the boys started to get tired. They began tending to the boys who needed a rest; after all, their knowledge and ambition could not be wasted either. By the time they had attended to and bandaged everybody, it had become pitch dark. Amidst the excitements of the great war, they completely forgot about the parents. In the end, naturally, they had to leave the battlefield in the middle of the Uzh the same way they came. They became just as wet as in the morning, except that the water had become much colder. Each of the gangs decided that they had won, that was why both gangs dashed home shouting hurrah.

The games our children played never involved expensive toys. In a neighboring courtyard belonging to a gardener there was a garage, and the children were allowed to climb on the roof. That served as the house for the girls: they would "cook" there, or sew dolls' dresses. One of their favorite games was playing "wedding." They collected old curtains and fancy dresses that weren't being used, and dressed up beautifully and went around the neighborhood, sometimes the whole street, inviting people to a wedding. Another time they brought home building materials from a neighboring builder's yard—bricks, cement, and whatever else was necessary—and they built a perfect little factory in the courtyard.

They also had stranger pastimes. Our house was opposite the cemetery of Uzhhorod, the famous Kapos Street cemetery. Our children followed the funeral rites with great interest; in fact, it became their hobby to participate in them. When they heard a funeral procession approaching, they dropped whatever they were doing and ran after it.

Hungarian funerals took place in silence, only the wheels of the ornamental hearse clattered on the cobble-stones. When the gang of children heard that sound, they darted immediately to the street. Slavic funerals were louder. The open coffin was carried on a truck, to the accompaniment of roaring music. My children still mention with horror that Slavs (local Rusyns as well as Ukrainians and Russians) always kissed the corpse on the lips before the coffin was closed. Gypsy funerals were the most lively and the most colorful. The deceased was always accompanied by a huge crowd and a large band supplemented with a drummer. For the procession, the band would play a Gypsy funeral march. At the grave, however, they always played the favorite song of the deceased, no matter how cheerful it was. The kids had become real experts of various funeral rites, and we also had to learn certain things because of them. When I could not find them and someone told me there was a Protestant funeral across the street, I would not expect them for a while, because a Protestant funeral took at least one hour and a half.

The cemetery inspired the kids also to more fearful amusements. In the evenings they scared cemetery-goers, wrapped in sheets and holding a candle put into a carved pumpkin, hooting in a ghostly voice. I must say, the effect was sometimes overwhelming.

All in all, our children's company consisted of nice, well-bred, good-mannered kids. They were mainly Hungarians: two Behun boys, two Böhm boys, three Teke girls, Sanyi Pricsni, two Kertész children, and my kids. A very nice Russian family, too, lived among us on Kapos Street. Their daughters learned Hungarian very well, and they also belonged to the gang. They, however, soon moved back to Leningrad, where they had come from.

Except for the Behuns, who were well-to-do cabinetmakers, every family was very poor. Despite this fact, every child's birthday was celebrated with a party. I took Lia and Öcsi to birthday parties outside Kapos Street as well. For example, we made friends with the family of our dentist, who had ten beautiful children. They were charming birthday parties, attended also by the moms. We had a nice chat together, and we came to know one another. Consequently, we did not worry whose home our children were playing at; we were sure they were at a decent place. At the birthday parties we served "floating islands," cakes, sandwiches and lemonade. We lived within our means, and whatever our means were, we did not give in to poverty. We had a good time and we ensured a harmonious life for our children.

When Sanyi also started to work again, we began to live better, especially while I worked at the center of the commercial cooperative, where I had access to a little extra food. Unfortunately, however, my asthma kept tormenting me. I could endure less and less the rush beginning early in the morning, and going on until late at night. My mother-in-law was also fed up that I was never at home, that keeping the house and minding the children were left to her alone. I had to change jobs, and so I became a cashier at the National Bank. I worked at the income cash-desk, where taxes of large amounts were paid in. In those days everybody was taxed for everything, so I had to tend to plenty of customers. In a very short time I learned to count in Russian and everything else I needed to communicate with the customers. Otherwise I did not know the language. My work was very tiresome, but at least I was finished by four o'clock. Sanyi also worked until four, so our family life returned to a normal track.

The fits of asthma came at the most unexpected moments, without any premonitory signs. They incapacitated me at work. I would choke until the fit was over. Of the cough relievers I took, one had an adverse effect on my eyes and the other on my heart. Whereas my asthma did not improve at all, my general condition worsened. I had fits practically every day, but I felt worst at night. My father-in-law worked as a night watchman at a building-yard established on a neighboring lot. During my nightly bouts, when I would pace back and forth, I often relieved him at the building-yard, saying: why should both of us stay up. After a night spent walking, naturally, one could not accomplish a responsible job demanding concentration. My ability to work became seriously impaired.

The employees of the National Bank, including both native Uzhhorod citizens and new settlers, formed an excellent team despite their mixed background and their large number. We began to get used to the situation that had come about; Hungarians, Ukrainians, and Russians worked together in harmony. We got along better and better with each other, although friendly chit-chat was limited only to the working hours. Those who learned Russian well at the language courses could be promoted as far as a chief accountant, despite their nationality. Our bosses also treated us well.

The leaders of the Bank granted me a month's leave at a sanatorium, hoping that it would be beneficial for my asthma. The sanatorium operated in a former manor house at Beregvár, near Mukachevo. I passed the month pleasantly, mainly in the company of acquaintances from Uzhhorod, in beautiful surroundings, even if I could not get used to Russian eating habits. Breakfast was the main meal of the day, with heavy, greasy meat courses, but I could only drink tea and perhaps eat some bread and butter in the morning. Since bread was given freely, I saved for later between slices of bread the meat and cheese served for breakfast. At lunchtime we had a light meal with compote, and in the evening we were given cream of wheat. We supplemented the sanatorium meals with fresh fruit, which was sold by peasants from the village below. I was treated very well up there, but my condition did not improve. By Christmas of 1948 I had stopped working altogether; I was not able to.

My sister-in-law and her husband had been among the first shopkeepers to have their shop expropriated. They had also divorced since then, and my sister-in-law had married András with whom she lived in

their old house. My former brother-in-law, Cirill, had been appointed
the manager of another shop before he became a joiner in a plywood
factory. Fortunately, he divorced only his wife. He did not turn his back
on our entire family. He helped us a lot! He would always let me know
if they expected sugar the following day, or if it looked like there would
be some other procurement possibility. It was out of the question for
me simply to go into his shop before or after the regular hours. Shop
managers were all under strict control, lest they should be involved in
illegal dealings. I was let into the closed shop because I was the one
who counted the income after closing. My help was really needed as
the accounts had to be settled before the bank's van arrived to collect
the money. That was how I sometimes obtained a little sugar, flour, or
semolina.

If we had no help of this kind, then procurement went on in the
following manner: one of us planted himself or herself in front of the
shop already at dawn. Then, after an hour, another member of the family replaced him so that he should not get frozen, and it went on like
that for hours, often for half a day. We had to stand in a queue for
everything. It happened frequently that the thing for which we queued
up had sold out just before it was our turn. Actually, this still happens
today, as well. My poor husband often comes home empty-handed. He
stands in the queue, honestly waiting his turn—he always queues up
honestly, without trying to be crafty—and by the time he gets to the
counter, there is no milk or sour cream left.

After the ruble was introduced, everyday life became very cheap.
We barely had to pay anything at all for the water or the electricity, and
we shopped for kopecks ("pennies") in the food store as well—provided there was something to buy. In those days, a cashier earned 36
rubles a month, an accountant 40 rubles, a qualified chief accountant
55 rubles, and a director 100 rubles. At the same time, a liter of milk
cost 20 kopecks, a loaf of bread 14 kopecks, and a pound of pork 80
kopecks. Underpants could be bought for 27 kopecks, a pair of socks
for the children for 20 kopecks, and a pair of stockings for myself for
90 kopecks. It was not easy to make ends meet, but neither was it impossible.

No matter how meager supplies were, I tried to provide healthy and
varied food and drinks for the family. Kvas was always available, but I
did not like it. After Coca-Cola, you would not want it. I was content
with tea. I bought milk for the kids, and sometimes I also made hot

chocolate. We prepared and bottled for winter grape juice, raspberry juice, and brambleberry juice. The sodawater with which we diluted the juice cost next to nothing. The introduction of sodawater changed the look of the city: in the large gateways built for double-doors, soda kiosks opened, one after the other. They employed the same kind of glass-rinser that dentists use. Their glass-rinsers fascinated me—in spite of the fact that I was an American girl! I also preserved and bottled fruit and pickles, and made jam. Tropical fruits were available in one year, and never after, but that year we had plenty of them. The Russians were not familiar with bananas and did not buy them. We ate a lot of them that winter—luckily, because then we did not see them again. Pomegranates from the Caucasus was available every winter, but we could not afford them. Now that trade is free again everything is available—for the minority who have money.

The choice and quality of milk products was not at all bad: there was milk, yoghurt, cottage cheese, and delicious butter. Little Lia's favorite was cocoa butter. It was similar to today's chocolate creams, but it was not sweetened, so it tasted even better. Sanyi loves Russian black bread, but I dislike it; however, I loved their rolls and croissants. Nowadays we eat Hungarian bread. It is brought across the border from Nyíregyháza every day. In the fifties we could buy palm-sized slices of the best cakes for 20 kopecks. Since then, confections have become less and less good and more and more expensive.

As far as alcohol is concerned, our family was lucky not to have been afflicted by it. But after Uzhhorod became part of the Soviet Union, alcoholism spread immeasurably. In the old days alcohol was readily available among Hungarians and Rusyns. Rusyns made brandy from damaged fruit, and they certainly drank it, too, but I never saw them drunk!

My husband was an ardent angler. On weekends he went fishing at dawn. Later in the morning we also packed up and followed him, and angling turned into a family excursion. We all love fish! Unfortunately, Sanyi took an interest in mushroom gathering only in his old age. Our friends often accompanied us on our excursions, and we frequently had visitors in the city, too. Together with constantly standing in queues, we had a great social life.

I made friends with Manyika Magyar and her sister Kati, while I was working in the center of the commercial cooperative. They often invited us to their place, where they entertained guests nearly constantly.

We liked to play cards together: rummy and "jolly seven." Their mother Ilona Magyar was the center of the company. She was constantly organizing excursions, parties, and games, but she also liked to be the hostess at name-day parties or at dinners following a pig slaughter. She collected friends and relatives around her as a hen collects her chicks. Our work places also organized social programs, but we did not take part in them. We were content with the social life of our own circle.

Besides the people surrounding Ilona Magyar, we saw a great deal of my husband's old friends, the Bertics boys. They lived in the second house from ours. They and Sanyi practically grew up together. The Berticses rarely left their house because they ran a thriving florist shop and plant nursery at home. Customers could go there to buy flowers, wreaths, etc., at any time of the day. When my asthma forced me to stop working at the bank, suddenly I had a lot of time but little money. So I occasionally worked for the Berticses. For example, I bedded plants in their greenhouse. Margitka, Mrs. Bertics, used to sell the nurslings at the market. Once Jóska Bertics asked me whether I felt like accompanying Margit to the market. He would take a box of nurslings for me to sell, as well. He offered me a decent percentage of the price. I gladly agreed: I had time for it, I sincerely enjoyed the market, and I also earned well.

One summer I was hawking at the market when a customer came up to me rejoicing: "My dear, I have been looking for you for such a long time! Earlier I used to buy nurslings from the Berticses, and they never turned out right. Those I bought from you last year, on the other hand, all have taken root." Margitka and I had a good laugh about it. Apparently, my nurslings indeed turned out well, and I began to collect a circle of loyal customers. The Berticses gave me work from spring to fall for several years.

We came to like the weekend markets and the Thursday second-hand fairs—two islands in the flood of state-control—so much so that we went there even when we did not have to. The company I regularly kept at the Thursday second-hand fairs included, for example, a friend of mine who was married to a well-to-do man and did not need any extra income at all. Still, she invariably joined us just for the fun of it. We laughed together when we managed to foist some junk off on somebody, or when we came across my nightgown in the street. Later, in harder times, after my husband had been taken away, the second-hand fairs became an important means for our survival. We emptied our wardrobes and parted with whatever nice things we still had.

Before the war I was very much content with my life. Teachers were well respected, and a teacher's salary provided a comfortable living for a family of four. Therefore we did not have the least intention of leaving the country. During the war I was glad if I could organize our life from day to day; and, of course, we were waiting for Sanyi to come home. It was out of the question to leave then. By the time we were all together again, and we realized that there was great trouble, it had become impossible to leave the country. I still tried anyway! I wanted to take my family to America!

CHAPTER 15

D espite my failure in Prague, my parents did not give up on us. They sent us invitations in 1947. They filled in all the necessary forms and paid all the necessary fees. The rest of the formalities had to be arranged at the American Embassy in Moscow. Naturally, we could leave our zone only with permission, and further permission was needed to enter Moscow. I saw no chance of my getting these permits, therefore I did not even try. I did not want to fall through at the first step. It seemed best for me to pretend that I was not aware of the zoning system.

In those years sports began to assume an extraordinary role in the Soviet Union, and they began to receive exceptional support, since they were seen as a means of showing to the world the strength, skill, and perseverance of the Soviet people. A friend of ours, a sportsman called Pista, was just about to go to Moscow to attend to some sports affairs. I joined him, pretending that we were a couple. He did have the proper documents, and we hoped this would be enough for both of us. My scheme worked perfectly on the way to Moscow. We took a direct flight, and nobody checked us at any point. Apparently, they assumed that no one would dare to leave for Moscow without being allowed to.

In Moscow Pista put me up with his friends: two single women with a little girl. They lived in the way most families did in Russian cities. They had a room off a long corridor, and shared a kitchen with all the other families living in the other rooms off the same corridor. Pista's friends received me cordially, despite their cramped circumstances. They also explained to me where I would find the American Embassy.

The next morning Pista accompanied me to the Embassy. It was guarded by both Soviet and American soldiers. Otherwise there was not a single person in sight. The situation is very different nowadays. One has to wait for days to get in! On presenting my invitation I was let in immediately, and I was received in a very polite way. They had already known about us, because Mommy and Daddy had arranged everything in advance. On the third day I got all the necessary documents. I took a photo of all four of us along. We were given a joint passport. Each of us had a separate page in it. The passport issued by the American Embassy would have entitled us, including Sanyi, to enter the United States. There was one stumbling block left: we also needed permission from the Soviet authorities before leaving the Soviet Union. This had to be applied for in Uzhhorod.

Pista had also settled his affairs in Moscow, so we set out for home. There were no airplane tickets available, so we took a train to Kiev. There we changed to a night train to Uzhhorod. Both Pista and I were asleep in our compartment when at a station somewhere between L'viv and Kiev we were awakened by an infernal hullabaloo. There was a hideous row on the platform, and a great hustling and bustling and jostling inside. Suddenly the conductor began shouting that everybody should check their luggage because someone's luggage had been thrown off the train. I looked around, and all my luggage was missing! I had been robbed of all my belongings! As it turned out, nobody else had anything missing! The train was about to leave. We got off to look for my luggage, but by that time everybody and everything had disappeared from the platform. As if nothing had happened! As if it had merely been a nightmare! And the American passport obtained under such great difficulties was gone! We went to the police. After all, I had been robbed of official documents of great importance. The police made a record of our complaint, but nothing else happened. In low spirits, we looked for another train and left for Uzhhorod again.

Afterwards, when I thought carefully about what had happened, I had no doubts that it was a carefully designed robbery, carried out very well, the purpose of which was to obtain our passport. The thieves knew very well that my luggage contained an American passport. During the whole distracting scene only my luggage was stolen, even though it did not look like something worth stealing at all. I was extremely distressed by the events. I informed the American Embassy of them, as well.

I was not only robbed of my passport; my local passport and my work-book also disappeared. I had to apply for new documents at the Uzhhorod police. At the police station, they sprang the question on me how I had reached Moscow without permission. I put on an innocent air, and explained to them with eyes round with astonishment that I simply had had business to do in Moscow, so I had gone there. "Don't you know it is forbidden?" they asked, and they could not believe their ears: "How could I have known! I lived in America, in Czechoslovakia, in Hungary, and in each of these countries I could travel to the capital whenever I wanted to. Why couldn't I do the same in the Soviet Union?" I have rarely seen policemen cheer up so much. Perhaps they did not make an issue out of my offence because I managed to make them laugh. I was fined and was given new documents. Nevertheless, I became ill from the matter.

In about half a year I was notified by the American Embassy that our passport would be renewed. It was my parents who had applied for the renewal, paying all the fees all over again. So in the spring of 1948 I set out again for Moscow, naturally without permission this time as well. I could not risk being refused right from the start.

A confectioner we knew well and his family also had relatives in America and also wanted to start the process of their emigration. Since such matters could be arranged more efficiently in Moscow, they asked me to act for them, too. They baked me two poundcakes and a box of walnut cookies for the journey. That was all I took along besides the necessary documents. This time I took a train. The Russian long-distance trains were very convenient and very clean. I shared a sleeping compartment with another passenger, also bound for Moscow. My fellow traveler proved to be a pleasant companion, so this journey also started well.

From the station I went directly to the Embassy. Again, I was let in right away; the receptionist already recognized me. Naturally we spoke in English. I enjoyed using my mother tongue after so many years. They asked me how long I could stay. When they learned that I was in a hurry because I had no lodging in Moscow, they put me up in the basement of the Embassy. I met several families there who were already waiting for their flight to America. I dwelt on the thought that I would soon be waiting there together with my family for the departure of our plane, as well. I left the building of the Embassy only for a few minutes to buy some ice cream at a kiosk at the next corner so as to supplement my diet of walnut cookies.

When my passport was ready, an Embassy car took me to the railway station. As soon as they left me alone, I was surrounded by policemen and taken to the police station. I happened to be eating ice cream, and I did not stop licking it! I ate every bit of it; I decided I would not let myself be disturbed while eating ice cream. They interrogated me thoroughly about what I was doing in Moscow. I told them everything, and apparently they accepted my answers and let me go. I got on my train and arrived in Uzhhorod without any incidents. There, however, the authorities were already waiting for me at the railway station. I was taken to the Uzhhorod police station right away where I was interrogated about where I had been and what I had been doing. "I have been to Moscow, and it was not the first time for me! I went to Moscow to pick up my American passport!" "What are your plans?" they asked. "I will apply for permission for us to leave the country." They let me submit my application, filling out an incredible number of forms and attaching an incredible number of fee stamps. They took the forms, registered them, and let me go.

Time wore on. More than half a year had already passed since I submitted the application, and still nothing had happened. I began to inquire, but there was no answer. Then Sanyi was arrested. That was how our "emigration" ended. I was desperate.

I felt sorry also for my poor parents. Not only did their wish to meet their daughther and their grandchildren not come true, but they also lost a lot of money. They were made to pay all the expenses of our immigration, including the flight tickets, and after the failure of our departure practically nothing was refunded to them. These events also tried them psychologically. When the United States turned out to be ready to take us, they were convinced there was no reason left why we should not be able to join them in America, and they were sure they could spend the rest of their lives together with us. Like other outsiders, they had no idea what the Soviet Union was like. They did not understand at all what was going on.

After a while they learned more about how we lived. If one could prove that one had a direct ancestor or descendant in Hungary, after waiting for half a year one could get a passport valid only to Hungary and only for a very limited period. Aunt Olga was one of the first lucky ones to get such a passport. She was allowed to visit her daughter, Gizike, in Budapest. Gizike corresponded with my parents, so through a series of linked transmissions Mommy got to know all the important news about us.

I had almost forgotten my first Moscow adventure already when I received a letter stating that the documents stolen from me had been found at a little railway station about one thousand kilometers from

Uzhhorod. We could go there to get them. Sanyi immediately said it was a trap, and we were not to go anywhere. If they had really wanted to return the documents to us, they would have sent them to Uzhhorod. Sanyi was convinced that if we went after the passport we would disappear like Wallenberg did, and our family would not even learn where we had been buried. So we did not react to the letter. We never heard anything about the documents ever again.

CHAPTER 16

A lthough my Sanyi never engaged in politics, never took part in any meetings, nor ever criticized the Soviet system in public, he did not have a quiet moment after the war. In 1948 it was already obvious to us that we were in danger. Our acquaintances began to disappear one after the other. First the priests were taken away, then the teachers and other intellectuals. We never knew what had happened to them. We only found that Gyurka was nowhere to be found, neither was another friend, nor a third one!

The teachers who were Sanyi's fellow soldiers in the deciphering battalion also began to disappear one by one, Rusyns and Hungarians alike. Sanyi noticed the interdependence of incidents with alarm. What was more, his acquaintances and colleagues began mentioning that "official" people, that is secret agents, were collecting information about him.

We felt the noose tightening around our necks. We went to work in the morning wondering if we would see each other again. Sanyi did not mind his own lot so much. He would say that once we had been born, we had to end our lives sometime. What worried him very much was my fate and the fate of the children. It drove him to despair that I, a girl growing up in peace, calm, and prosperity, had come here from America to live in constant terror and misery. He was also afraid that his children would have to grow up in destitution, without a father; what was more, at a disadvantage in a hostile world because of their father.

Sanyi worked hard at the commercial cooperative of the district. Owing to his honest work, he was promoted to technical manager, which was the second highest rank at the cooperative. In March he was ordered to give a "lecture of enlightenment" on atheism to the workers. My Sanyi, a devout, practicing Christian, leading an exemplary Christian life, was appointed to do that! Since our family belonged to more than one denomination, on Sundays we went to three churches, one after the other. First we took part in a Greek Catholic mass, then we went to a Roman Catholic mass, and eventually we attended a Lutheran service. We could get the children to take part in the third one only by promising them extra portions of ice cream afterwards. Sanyi told the party committee that he could not give a lecture on atheism since the workers had known him for all their lives and they would simply not believe him! He suggested that if it was indeed necessary, the task should be given to a person from the East; he would certainly be given more credit. Soon afterwards he was dismissed from his position without any explanation. It happened presumably because of the atheist lecture that he did not undertake, or maybe he just did not clap enthusiastically enough at the meetings for the cooperative.

The borders had been closed for good. There was no escaping from behind the iron curtain. Fear came upon us. We expected to be taken away any day. One of the signals was that Sanyi was called upon by his cooperative to quit his job. He loved his work and had been doing it in the most conscientious way possible. His bosses had always appreciated his work and had always been entirely satisfied with him. He had also been popular among his colleagues. His unmotivated dismissal indicated that there was, nevertheless, a great problem with him, a problem of a different kind.

At that time the cooperative was no longer led by András, our brother-in-law. "Distribution," which was to replace commerce, was performed by a pyramid of county cadres, district cadres, and local cadres. Each cadre was a Russian or Ukrainian newcomer. Even though my brother-in-law was a Ukrainian, and he himself had organized the whole commercial cooperative, he did not join the party, and without a party membership it was impossible to hold a high office. After the whole system of the cooperative had been built up and had been operating smoothly, internal security officers began to visit András, interrogating him about his past, his contacts. Then he was suddenly dismissed. It is possible that somebody else wanted his post. Fortunately, he found himself a lesser position in Mukachevo. Sanyi also managed to find other work. An old friend of his managed a little soft drink factory. He gave him a job in the office.

As another signal of the approaching catastrophe, I was called upon—as a foreign citizen—to go to the police to have my passport changed. I did not have the slightest intention of going there. I did not

98

want another passport. I was perfectly satisfied with the American passport I had. I did not react to the second notice, either, but the third time I had to obey. On the third occasion, the new document intended for me, the Soviet ID, was brought to our home. I was told emphatically that I had better take it in the interest of my family. Although I have never renounced my American citizenship, from that moment on the Soviets regarded me as a Soviet citizen. My nationality was given as "Slovak" because I was born in mother's village of Leles in Slovakia, even though I lived there only for a few months as a baby, and I did not speak a word of Slovak. It was then that I realized how the Soviet Union was manipulating its ethnic composition.

One morning I looked out of the window and noticed that three passports (passport is the Russian word used for an ID) were thrown into the flower garden in front of our house. Sanyi went out to look at them. To our alarm, they were passports valid for the first zone. One needed permission even to enter the second zone, to which Uzhhorod belonged; the first zone along the border was totally inaccessible. The obvious provocation was a sign of imminent disaster. Sanyi put the documents on the top of the cupboard, and we waited to meet our fate. We did not have to wait long.

In vain I accepted the Soviet passport for my family's sake. A week after I had been appointed a Soviet citizen Sanyi was arrested. It was July 2, 1949, the day of our eleventh wedding anniversary. Sanyi naturally had a valid passport. He was called to the police on the pretext that certain data related to his military service still remained to be filled in. He was ordered to go to the *militsiia* of the 2nd district. He hesitated about whether or not he should go there. Eventually he came to the conclusion that whatever he did, he had no way to escape anyway. I accompanied him to the door of the police station. I was not the only one to do so; we were followed by two men ever since we left our house. When Sanyi entered, I could not go with him any further. The guard told me nothing but *seichas, seichas* (in a moment).

Our neighbors knew what was going on with us. They knew that Sanyi was being kept in, and I was not being told anything. Margit Teke came to me with the idea that a friend of hers had an apartment opposite the militsia, and from her window one could look right into the militsia offices. Perhaps we might be able to find out something. So we went up to her place, and we saw from her window that Sanyi was sitting at a table, engaged in a conversation. Afterwards I learned that the boss was not inside, and they were waiting for him at that table. In any case, they were talking so peacefully that we calmed down. We waited for the end of the conversation. We saw him stand up, and start going downstairs together with his escorts. Once downstairs, he was led to a large black car waiting there. Two huge men whisked him inside, and he was driven away. I became paralyzed with panic. Everyone knew that the "black raven," the infamous *chornyi voron* was the car of the local unit of the NKVD, the Soviet secret police, called Bezpeka in Ukrainian. My Sanyi was taken to the prison (*tiur'ma*) of the Bezpeka!

I confirmed later that Sanyi had been detained at the Bezpeka. Every person carried away by the authorities ended up there. Besides, the family members of those affected shared with one another everything they could find out, and they informed me that Sanyi was there. Officially we were not informed of anything. They did not condescend to let the families know where their husband, father, mother, child was. My Sanyi enjoyed the "hospitality" of the Bezpeka for six weeks during the time of his interrogation.

On the second day of Sanyi's arrest our home was raided by the police. They searched it very thoroughly. Fortunately, the children were at school, so they were spared those shocking and humiliating scenes. They found nothing that was politically incriminating except for the passports that they themselves had planted in our garden. In fact, they barely found anything at all, we were so poor. They did not like my book of prayers, and also treated my handwritten book of recipes with suspicion. They ordered me to hand over to them all the personal belongings of Sanyi, as well as his photos from the family album. I flatly refused, saying they have Sanyi in his entirety. We, on the other hand, only have these photos, so I would not give them up! I also refused to part with his belongings. "I will have to sell all his clothes to be able to feed my children!" I said. "You cannot take anything away! It is because of you that I am left here with two children and with no breadwinner!" I don't know what gave me so much pluck; somehow it came naturally. It must have been the audacity one feels at the end of the world, when nothing matters anymore. In any case, nothing was taken away from us—perhaps because of my astounding conduct—even though they liked to confiscate things in those years.

Poor Sanyi received his salary just before his arrest. Amidst the great excitement it did not come to our mind that he should take the money out of his pocket. From the Bezpeka he could not send it to us any more. We were left with no father, no husband, and no money. As for Sanyi's fate, I learned what he actually went through from him six years later. He was taken down to the cellar of the Bezpeka headquarters. His watch, his American Parker pen, his Parker pencil, and his belt were taken away from him. He was lucky enough to have a guard who did not steal the 19 rubles he found in Sanyi's pocket, but asked Sanyi what he should buy him for his money. My Sanyi was a heavy smoker, and was suffering from the lack of cigarettes. He asked the guard to spend all of the 19 rubles on cigarettes. The guard did so, and the following day he brought Sanyi 19 rubles worth of the "Verhovina" brand. As Sanyi told me later, his nervous tension disappeared as soon as he knew himself to be in possession of such a significant stock of cigarettes.

His cell contained nothing but a bunk, without a blanket or anything. More precisely, there was also a 100-watt light bulb, which was constantly lit, day and night. My poor husband suffered most from the bedbugs, which was mysterious because there was absolutely no bedding, no furniture, nothing in there, and the light was also constantly on! Still, when he could not continue pacing back and forth any longer, and collapsed on his bunk, the Bezpeka's bedbugs immediately came forth from somewhere and they would bite him till they drew blood. Sanyi was kept in this underground hole for three days, without anybody saying a word to him. He was given salted fish and water, and he was watched through the the peep-hole (*fortochka*), but nothing else happened.

On the fourth day, the door of his solitary cell opened up and the Bezpeka guard led Sanyi into cell 13. Cell 13 was already occupied by six prisoners: three Greek Catholic priests, two village notaries, and a former Hungarian gendarme. Sanyi found their company a relief; he had good conversations with them. It turned out though that it was advisable to be careful when conversing with others. After the fourth week, a man called Kotrozs was brought into their cell. Sanyi happened to know him because Kotrozs had been the head of a unit of their commercial cooperative. He had embezzled 260,000 rubles, for which he was sentenced to ten years in prison. They found it strange that a non-political offender should be placed among them, because political and non-political offenders were not mixed together at the Bezpeka yet. For a whole day, Kotrozs tried to strike up a conversation with the priests, then with the others at least. He was thrown in there to gather information, but without any success. His provocations were so obvious that none of the captives was taken in.

In cell 13 the bunk also had a straw mattress, a straw pillow, and a blanket to go with it. Despite this fact, there were no bedbugs! On the other hand, there was a slop-pail in the corner. The prisoners were never allowed to leave their cell, unless they were taken to be interrogated. They received salted fish for meals. Water, on the other hand, was often forgotten about. If they were taken to be interrogated before they finished their water, the water had disappeared by the time they were taken back. They were allowed to sit on their beds, but they could not lie down. They were constantly checked through the peep-hole. Whereas during the day it was forbidden to lie down, during the night they were dragged off to be interrogated. Perhaps the greatest strain for them was that they were not allowed to sleep. A victim worn out to the utmost was certainly easier to handle.

Sanyi related to me later how his nights were spent. At six p.m. a guard came for him and escorted him to his interrogator. He was made to sit on a stool and stay there motionless, with his hands behind his back. The interrogating officer would fiddle with things and read as if Sanyi was not there. Hours went by. When my husband started to stir because he could not stand it to be motionless any longer, the interrogator rang for the guard, who took him back to cell 13. At night it was possible to lie down, so Sanyi tumbled on his bed and immediately fell into deep sleep. Ten minutes later the guard shook him awake, and took him to the interrogator again. He was so exhausted that he did not even know where he was. He had to sit down again with his hands behind his back, and then the officer began to ask him questions. The officer also wrote down certain things, but clearly not what Sanyi said. Later he shoved the sheets of paper into Sanyi's hand, and told him to read them and sign them. "I trust you," Sanyi said, and signed every sheet without reading it. He knew that if he did not sign the "minutes," the interrogator would sign them for him. If he did not protest but signed everything without any resistance, then he could go back to his cell and if there was something left of the night, then he could sleep at last. In those weeks, his only ambition was to be able to sleep. He was barely allowed to at all! And the interrogation went on like this every night for six weeks. Custody pending trial could only last for six weeks, and by that time a sentence had to be produced.

The interrogator reinterpreted what Sanyi said in a particular way. They attributed to him, as one of his main crimes, work as an instructor in the Levente movement, a paramilitary youth organization in Horthy-ruled Hungary. My poor Sanyi told his interrogator that he had been called up by the army, otherwise he would not have had anything to do with the Levente, and he was appointed as a help to a main Levente instructor because he was a teacher by profession. He had to hold gymnastics classes for the Levente; he practiced at most "right turn, left turn, about-turn" with them. The minutes of the interrogation naturally contained the officer's version, according to which Sanyi as a Levente instructor educated the youth in the spirit of fascism, and incited them to fight against the Bolshevik power. Poor Sanyi said in vain that Bolshevism was never even touched on during the gymnastics classes.

The main charge against Sanyi was that in his capacity as a radio cipher officer of the former Hungarian army, he was spying against the Soviet Union. Furthermore, he was a lieutenant, the commander of a whole unit. According to the minutes, by deciphering secret military telegrams he provided direct help to the German chiefs of staff. He said in vain that he was an officer of the Hungarian army, not the German one, and he was not a volunteer but was called up. He had not wished for the war; he would not have left his beautiful, young wife and two young children alone if he had not had to. He joined the army because he was forced to. Besides, he did not really decipher secret telegrams. He translated Morse code signals into numbers. He had no idea what the telegrams meant. Whatever Sanyi said, the minutes were prepared according to the interrogator's intentions.

At the Bezpeka, the prisoners were allowed to receive a food parcel (*peredacha*) once a week. It was simpler for the Bezpeka, too, if their prisoners were fed by their families. Meeting with a prisoner was naturally out of the question. We merely gave the parcel to the guard and told him who it was for. It was hopeless to hide a message in the food, because they checked everything thoroughly. They cut up the dumplings, opened the stuffed cabbages, they even broke the cigarettes into two. When they saw that we did not attempt to smuggle anything in, they began to deliver my parcels to Sanyi in a better condition. I always prepared for him what I thought he lacked the most: some soup, cookies, and plenty of cigarettes. A captive could only get his food parcel if he "behaved well," i.e., if he signed everything. Stubborn men, who stuck to the truth, did not get anything. Sanyi was not stubborn. He found there was no point in it. He found sleep and parcels more important. He shared the parcels he got with the others. They were appreciated more than salted fish.

We women gathered in front of the Bezpeka around six in the morning, and waited for new developments until about nine at night. In the meantime we became acquainted with each other. I got to know the wives of several priests and teachers, some of whom became my friends. Manci, the wife of a teacher, and Bella, the wife of a lawyer, came to Uzhhorod every day from Antalovtsi (Hungarian: Antalóc) and Berehovo (Beregszász), respectively, to stand out in front of the Bezpeka. We made life easier for each other. I put them up, and in return they brought chickens and other cooking materials from the country. In the evening, when we went home after having spent the day waiting and hoping, we cooked the meal, leaving some for the children. Then we slept for a few hours and set off for the Bezpeka again. They never told us anything. If someone had been transferred from the Bezpeka, we learned it from the fact that his parcel was not accepted.

My children and I were left with 3 rubles and 60 kopecks. It was then that I began to knit sweaters to sell so as to have some income. I used the time I spent standing in front of the Bezpeka to knit for money. The children knew where their daddy was, but they did not ask why. They only kept asking when he would come home.

It took six weeks to prepare the indictment, which made up a thick book. After the day of the trial was set, I was allowed to hire a lawyer as counsel. The lawyer asked for 200 rubles for the defense. I sold my gold jewelry and all my other possessions that could be turned into cash. It was incredibly difficult to scrape together that huge amount. The lawyer assured me that he visited Sanyi regularly and consulted with him often. I found it strange, though, that he did not tell us anything about the case. We had no idea what Sanyi was accused of, why he was in custody to begin with, and when the trial would take place. We only knew what we found out ourselves while standing out in front of the Bezpeka all day long, week after week. Having cheated us of all we possessed, the lawyer kept swearing that everything would be all right with Sanyi. Instead, Sanyi got the heaviest sentence possible. Six years later Sanyi and I pieced together what he went through and what I experienced. It was then that Sanyi learned from me that he had a hired counsel, and it was then that I learned from Sanyi that he had never even seen the lawyer. Although we paid the lawyer 200 rubles, he and his like counselled the authorities, not the defendants.

A series of trials took place every day. Even if the families were not notified, we knew when a person was to be tried and sentenced. Our trial was early in the fall. It took place at the county court, behind closed doors. Besides the judge, the attorney, and the two lay judges (the so-called "people's judges"), only the witnesses could enter the room. The "witnesses" brought against Sanyi included two peasants from Turia Bystra, who alleged that in 1944 Sanyi preached the victory of the Germans and the defeat of the Soviets in front of the Turia Bystra church. It was obvious that they were false witnesses. Sanyi never discussed politics in public to begin with, and in 1944 he could not have said such things in private, either. The English had already bombed out the German industry, the Soviets were already inside Hungary. No person in his right mind could have thought that Germany would win! Sanyi actually asked the attorney if he really thought him to be that stupid. A former fellow soldier of Sanyi's, Gyurka Gyümölcs, who had been arrested two months earlier, was brought to bear witness against Sanyi after he had been sentenced to twenty-five years. He had to testify that Sanyi was a cipher officer in the 101st reconnaissance battalion of the Hungarian army. However, Sanyi had never denied that!

At the trial, all the nonsense that Sanyi had already known from the interrogations was repeated to him. What he had to say did not matter in the least, just like during the interrogations. On the basis of his past as a Hungarian officer and a Levente instructor, he was declared to be an enemy of the Communist system, a spy, and a criminal. When the judgment was read out at the end of the trial, Sanyi's hair literally stood on end.

People of a similar background were convicted on the basis of two articles. One of them imposed ten years in prison, the other one twenty-five years. It was unpredictable which poor wretch would fall into the ten-year category, and which one into the other. Actually, one could obtain a ten-year sentence just by refusing to spy on one's neighbors. A colleague and good acquaintance of Sanyi's, Laci Ivaskovics, a teacher from Antalovtsi, was ordered to keep an eye on the mail arriving at his village. Laci refused to do so, and he received a ten-year sentence!

The teachers from Sanyi's deciphering battalion who had been tried before him all got twenty-five years. Gyurka Gyümölcs was first sentenced to death, but his sentence was changed to twenty-five years after the abolishment of the death penalty. My poor husband also expected that much. His prospects were aggravated, in addition, by his American wife. For whatever reason, he received twenty-five years. A twenty-five-year sentence did not simply mean twenty-five long years. It meant that we would never see each other again. He would never again be able to hug his children! If Stalin had not died, the prisoners would never have returned! The huge Gulag archipelago needed an infinite number of people. Not even those who served their sentences were ever given permission to return home. Sanyi met Ukrainians there who were taken to the Gulag in 1931 and who had completed their sentence a long time before, but still they were not allowed to go home. They had to settle down in the taiga. The authorities did not expect to be able lure volunteers to work there as shopkeepers, stock keepers, etc., so these jobs, which they did not entrust to prisoners, were given to ex-prisoners forced to stay.

I found out Sanyi's sentence when he was led out of the courtroom. He showed twenty-five with his fingers. I could see him only as long as he was being led along the corridor, and I had to behave quietly, despite the twenty-five years! The corridor of the county court was the only place where we could be in contact with our loved ones, during breaks in the trial. As the women who spent their days waiting around the Bezpeka, the court, and the municipal prison found out, if one lurked silently in the corridor leading to the courtroom, she would not be driven away. When the prisoner was led out to the toilet, his relative could even slip in with him. The success of these attempts depended on who was on guard because there were milder and stricter guards. I managed to slip into the toilet twice. Once I could even replace my husband's shoes with a pair of more convenient, heavy-duty ankle boots. It was when I learned about the twenty-five years that I saw my dear Sanyi for the last time!

After the sentence Sanyi was not taken back to the Bezpeka headquarters but was transferred to the regular prison of Uzhhorod. The municipal prison was different from the Bezpeka cellar. Those sentenced to ten years or fewer lived on the lower stories behind doors that were closed but had no chains, and they had ordinary iron beds. The prisoners sentenced to more than ten years, staying on the upper stories, had doors that closed with two chains in addition to the lock. For a bed they had an unmovable "coffin" made out of thick, heavy oak, which also had a mattress, a pillow, and a blanket. The window below the ceiling was covered so that it let some light in from outside, but it did not let the prisoner look out.

In the municipal prison prisoners were allowed to get a parcel every day, and I tried to procure something delicious for each parcel. In our civil relations we were not ostracized. On the contrary, everybody tried to help us. The Demeter family (the parents of my friend Csöpike) still had a cow and sent along a liter of milk for the children every morning. Another friend of mine offered to put together Sanyi's food parcel every Thursday. For our sake she prepared a particularly rich and nourishing meal each Thursday: fried chicken, chicken in breadcrumbs, stuffed chicken, or something that could also be eaten cold.

We were not given any information by the municipal prison, either. There, too, the only indication of someone having been transferred was that his food parcel was not accepted. We women, however, were not put off so easily. We realized that the storm window in the loft of a certain house looked right onto the yard of the prison. From that time on we climbed to that loft every day and watched in silence to see who was there for his walk and who was not to be seen any longer. The walk took place in several turns; however, there was room only for one person at the loft window. Fortunately, we already knew one another's husbands by sight, so we could take turns at the window. I never managed to catch sight of Sanyi, but I let the others know if I saw their Gyurka or Iván walking. They also reported if Sanyi showed up. If someone disappeared, if he did not participate in the walks any longer, there was no knowing where he had been taken to. There were so many distribution centers that even the first station of a prisoner could be anywhere.

The Uzhhorod prison granted us visiting time once. I could only take Öcsi with me because little Lia was in a sanatorium. We just looked at each other and cried. Sanyi said only one thing to me. There was a general belief then that women who divorced their imprisoned husbands had a better chance to lead an undisturbed life. Sanyi urged me to divorce him. "No, never!" I answered. That was all we said to each other. Actually many women got a divorce, but that did not make life easier for them. Although they did not bear a "compromised" name any longer, their dignity broke. They were not given strength by loyalty and perseverance.

CHAPTER 17

I could have sworn that I saw Sanyi's head in the Black Maria [infamous black Soviet car used to convey prisoners] on November 1. My parcel for him was, indeed, returned to me the next day. I heard it second-hand that he had been taken to the transfer prison (*peresel'naia tiur'ma*) in L'viv. As I found out later, the conditions were relatively good in L'viv. The L'viv prisoners were given substantial, tasty meals. They usually had tomato soup with fish and various kinds of hearty second courses. According to Sanyi, all prisoners put on weight there without extra food from home. It was obvious why the food was so rich. The L'viv prison was a center where prisoners were distributed to prison camps. Slaves had to be fattened up so that they could endure the harrowing journey in the cattle trucks and the work they were to do in extremely hard conditions.

Since I did not know that they received good meals, I gave blood, and from the money that I was paid for it I filled Sanyi's old military backpack with salami, bacon, sweets, and cigarettes, and I left for L'viv. I did not have to go alone. Another prisoner's wife, Irén Kása, had her food parcel returned by the Uzhhorod prison the same day when my parcel was not accepted. She heard that her husband Jóska had also been taken to L'viv. He was sentenced to ten years for "black marketeering." Irén was also of the opinion that we should venture upon a trip to L'viv because perhaps we might still see them!

So Irén and I set out for L'viv. We chose the 7th and 8th of November, so that we would have to spend as few workdays on the trip as possible. We sat on the train from four p.m. until early the next morning among awful company. Traveling was pleasant only in the sleeping wagons, but in the sitting compartments the company was always unbearable.

In L'viv we asked the passers-by where the municipal prison was to be found. We walked there and began to look for some lodging in the neighborhood. We found a bedbug-infested room available in a private apartment. There were so many bedbugs in the room that at night we did not dare to go to bed. We just sat on the bed, huddled together. We accepted those awful circumstances because we wanted to be near the prison. Those who wanted to hand over a food parcel had to start standing in line at dawn. There was no time for us to waste the following morning.

We discovered a café nearby which was very clean, and they also sold wienerwurst. We went there twice a day. We explained to the manager of the café what we were doing in L'viv. On hearing the conditions we were living in, he allowed us to wash and to fix ourselves in the bathroom of the café. Each time he saw us enter, the little man would ask immediately: "The usual stuff?" "The usual stuff" meant a wienerwurst, a *bulochka* (a delicious baked bun), a cup of hot chocolate, an ice cream, and the use of the bathroom.

Both Irén and I asked for visiting time. She got it, but I did not. As it turned out, visits were granted only to those sentenced to ten years or fewer. Sanyi heard that I was there. It made him literally sick that he was nevertheless not able to see me. The food parcel I had brought for him, however, was let through. Poor Sanyi did not gain much by it! In the transfer prisons and camps political prisoners were already mixed together with nonpolitical offenders, including the most depraved, most violent criminals, who were ready to kill their fellow prisoner for a rich food parcel. There was no place to hide the food away, either. One hundred to two hundred prisoners were crammed into a single "cell" on three-decker bunks with no mattress or blanket. There was no place to save even the cigarettes. So he distributed everything that I bought for my blood, from the salamis to the last cigarette. One of his cellmates was Levente Székely, an Uzhhorod citizen who served in the former Hungarian army as a counter-intelligence chief of the rank lieutenant-colonel. After the upper class life he had been used to, he was in a most sorry state of mind amidst that miserable slavery. Sanyi gave him a salami as well.

After I had passed on the parcel and had been refused the visiting time, there was nothing left for me to do in L'viv. However, I did not want to leave Irén alone, so I waited with her until the day on which her visiting time was set. L'viv has many beautiful sights which would have been worth looking at, but we were mentally sick people and could not force ourselves to visit any of them even in the idle hours of waiting. We only went into a church to pray.

We were not interested in anything but our husbands and our families, who had to be provided for no matter what the conditions were. We lived in our own world. Our problems, achievements, and joys were different from those of others. We, the women concerned, understood each other perfectly. Other people, on the other hand, could not really comprehend our situation. However, despite the insurmountable gap, we constantly felt their solidarity. Most people, whether friends or passing acquaintances like the unknown coffeshop manager in L'viv, tried to help us as soon as they found out what had happened to us. As I see it now, this was a kind of resistance to the regime as well.

After Irén's visit was over, we took a train home. From that time on there was nothing we could do for our husbands. I fasted twice a week and prayed frequently, hoping that God would help us.

Sanyi's first letter came from L'viv. The next one in late December was sent from another large transfer camp already. In these transfer camps the prisoners collected from all over the country were grouped according to the demands of the labor camps of the Gulag. They were sent off once there were enough prisoners to make up a transport to a particular destination. Sanyi went through two transfer camps before he reached his end-station.

After a month spent in L'viv, Sanyi and his fellow prisoners were put into cattle trucks and were taken to Akimoka, a little Ukrainian village about a hundred kilometers from the Sea of Azov. German prisoners of war were building a highway there to connect Moscow to Symferopil' in the Crimea. They were to continue the work of the German POWs, who had to be relieved at the end of 1949. Yet the Akimoka labor camp, located in a comparatively pleasant area, was eventually filled by non-political offenders, and Sanyi and his fellow political prisoners were moved on to Dnipropetrovs'k.

In the Dnipropetrovs'k prison Sanyi shared the asphalt-lined cell with two hundred fifty-nine other prisoners. They were crammed into three-decker bunks so closely that if one of them wanted to turn, the others had to turn as well. Although there was no heating, still they were warm because of the crowded conditions, even in January and February, when the outside temperature dropped to between -28° and -32° centigrade. The steam and reek of bodies would belch through the ventilating window and then freeze outside. According to Sanyi, those who were not there simply cannot imagine the smell that filled the cell. Most unfortunately for Sanyi, his bed was on a bottom bunk by the door, where the *barsha* was set up. *Barsha* was the name of the device which they had to step on and squat over to relieve themselves, all two hundred and sixty people! In the morning, they were taken to wash themselves. In the lavatory they would wade up to the ankles through excrement mixed with urine and water. There were only five or six small faucets, and they had to rush so that everyone could have a turn at them. Fortunately, they received three substantial meals a day in Dnepropetrovsk.

Then they were given orders to prepare to leave. They were not told, however, where they would be taken. Some guessed they would go to the coal mines of Vorkuta. Others expected to be taken to Arkhangelsk to cut down timber. Half the country was still in ruins, so timber was in great demand.

They left after dark. They had to walk for a while before reaching the trucks. The prisoners were divided into groups of twelve. They marched in such a way that twelve prisoners were followed by twelve guards with twelve bloodhounds, then again twelve prisoners followed by twelve guards and twelve bloodhounds. Political prisoners were guarded as if they were the most depraved criminals! People in the streets stopped to look at the strange procession. Sanyi was convinced they thought they were looking at dangerous murderers. The prisoners were entrained in cattle trucks furnished with two-decker bunks and a *barsha*. The door was padlocked behind them. In the morning some bread and tea were thrown in. Then they did not get anything else for the rest of the day. Everyone was still wearing the clothes in which he was arrested. Sanyi had been arrested in July and was still wearing his light summer suit.

They traveled in the cattle truck for a whole week. They arrived in Arkhangelsk on the 1st of April. They waited there until the distribution of prisoners was completed, and then set out for their final destination: their permanent labor camp.

CHAPTER 18

After returning from L'viv I had to find some sort of livelihood.
Until then we scraped along with the help of friends. My friend
Csöpike and her family, who were well off, invited us for dinner
remarkably often. Mamuka also treated us to meals sometimes. Aunt
Olga, who also invited us for lunch every now and then, related to her
daughter living in Budapest what had happened to us, and her daughter
Gizike wrote everything to my parents. Mommy found out how they
could help us. She made a deal with Aunt Olga that they would support
Gizike financially in Budapest, and in return Aunt Olga would provide
us with dinner every day. So I only had to earn enough money to buy us
breakfast and supper, which I did at first mainly by knitting.

Knitted clothing was very easy to sell. In fact, I would knit to order,
so I could count on knitting as a permanent, safe source of income. I
discovered that more things could be unravelled and be knit from than
anyone would imagine. For example, I unravelled the American flour
sacks. Though the weft was made of paper, the warp could be used for
knitting. It was not easy to work with, though, for it cut my hands and
caused them to bleed. On the other hand, the beige-colored material
was very easy to dye. I knit excellent trousers from it for the winter. I
also used bandages cut into strips. I knitted baby jackets and baby caps
with them. They were tousled and frilly and they looked cute. I also
worked for peasant women from the country. They brought me their
old-fashioned shawls which I unravelled and reknit into sweaters. Years
later yarn reappeared in the shops. It was rather uneven, but it was pure
wool. I realized that if I knitted with prewashed wool, the sweater would
never change its shape. I knitted many, very many wonderful things
with it!

One fall knitted and crochet caps came into fashion. I looked at the
most fashionable forms, did some experimenting, and then I started
mass production. I showed the first sample pieces to my former col-

leagues in the National Bank. Each of them bought one. Then they also ordered mufflers to go with the caps. In the end, they even brought me the yarn, and I only had to do the knitting. By the time every woman had a cap, knitted hats came in, so I could begin to mass-produce knitted hats!

A friend of ours, Jóska, worked as the stock-keeper of the central iron wares warehouse of an industrial cooperative (the place where later I would also find a job). He was the one who issued the raw materials to the workshops. Occasionally I dropped in on Jóska and asked him for a handful of nails, or something else that I needed to solve some household problem. Once the warehouse received a huge consignment of waxed cloth. Several rolls arrived in lovely colors: red, yellow, brown, green, white, and black. Jóska had no idea what to do with them. No unit of the industrial cooperative used any waxed cloth. On the other hand, it did not occur to him—and it would not have occurred to anybody else—to return what he had been allotted. Everything was to be appreciated! Besides, a person who did not want his allocation was not given anything the next time.

A friend of mine had just been to Moscow, where she had bought a satchel-like red bag with a drawstring. It looked very good. I borrowed it, and took it to Olga, Jóska the stockkeeper's wife. Olga was very good at sewing. I showed her the bag, and asked her if, in her opinion, we could also make a similar one. She looked at it, and cut out the pattern immediately. We made a few test pieces of different colors and also lined them nicely. Then I put one on my shoulder and walked around in the city. Every woman I met stopped me and asked me where I had obtained that cute bag of mine, and if I could also get one for them. "I am not sure," I answered, "but I will try." And the news about the provenance of ladies' bags spread by word of mouth. Olga was kept busy for months, putting bags together. We used up the whole waxed cloth consignment of the warehouse. I received a decent percentage of the profits. Although I did not participate in the production, I was the creative source of the idea and I was the saleswoman. It was a product of unbelievable success, and it brought a nice income for both of us.

Before the Christmas of 1949, our first Christmas without Sanyi, we found another source of livelihood, too. In the streets young Gypsy girls were selling Christmas wrappings for candies to be hung on the Christmas tree. Lia looked at the wrappings, and came home with the idea that we could make much nicer ones. We tried, and indeed, we found that if we cut the edges while holding several pieces of paper together, then, when we pulled the sheets apart, the fringes became ruffled in a lovely way. We filled these wrappings with the cheapest sweets that could be bought and we had unbelievable success with them! We did nothing else for a whole week, and just could not make enough of them. To tell the truth, the paper for the wrappings came from the office of the cooperative. After we had been robbed by the State of everything we had, including the head of the family, I stopped having qualms about using up a little waxed cloth, a few nails, or some paper from the common property. We lived as we could. One sheet of paper was sufficient for two wrappings. They were so beautiful that not even today's Christmas wrappings could match them. We also presented our friends with sweets in Christmas wrappings. We made a boxful for each of them.

I also had extra income after I found regular work, thanks to my boss. There was a shortage of handkerchiefs in the city, and our cooperative decided to manufacture them. The handkerchiefs were cut and edged by a team of three. One of the paints available resisted washing fairly well; it did not fade. We used this paint to stripe the handkerchiefs by hand with a pipette. They let me have a bunch of handkerchiefs to stripe at home. This, naturally, meant that I did not sleep because I spent half of every night pipetting. The reasonable thing to do would have been to stripe as many handkerchiefs as possible in the shortest possible time, instead, I let my imagination run free and I kept changing the pattern, also because that way it was less boring. Little Lia also prepared lovely designs: different combinations of colors, of wide and narrow stripes, etc. We kept making them more and more beautiful until the others got fed up that only our handkerchiefs had any success. So my career as a handkerchief-decorator came to an end, but while it lasted, it meant good income. That was the way we lived, always embracing every opportunity we could.

It took me a lot of time and effort to find a regular job. Bosses tried to avoid employing prisoners' wives. The cooperative where I found work eventually was managed by a sweet Jewish man who did not forget what it had been like to be an outcast. His cooperative gave shelter to countless people in need. He also knew, of course, that we were the best workers available. The women who were left alone belonged to the most cultured families. After all, it was the priests, teachers, civil servants, the intelligentsia who had been systematically liquidated. The wife of a fate-stricken priest or teacher worked harder than anybody else. On the one hand, she wanted to keep her job, and she did not want to worsen the situation of her children and possibly that of her husband (if the situation of our husbands could be worsened at all). On the other hand, she was reliable by virtue of her education. My closest colleagues were a priest deprived of his profession but not deported for some reason, and four political prisoners' wives. We worked for very little money, but we were happy to be allowed to work at all.

Our cooperative employed many priests' wives, which was not an accident: the priests were among the first victims of the Soviet regime. The Greek Catholic church was hit the hardest. It was seen—with good reason—as the guard and symbol of Rusyn national identity and Subcarpathian cultural independence. It was totally banned in 1949 and this ban was effective until 1989. Rusyns were compelled to join the Orthodox church, with the intent to assimilate them to the Ukrainian nationality. Hungarian Greek Catholics, including the Greek Catholic members of our family, started going to a Roman Catholic church instead. Simultaneous with the ban on Greek Catholicism, the Greek Catholic clergy was effectively eliminated. Priests could choose between converting to Orthodoxy or being deported. The exact data concerning what had happened to them came to light only a short while ago. About a third of the three hundred and fifty Greek Catholic priests of Subcarpathia converted, although some did so only nominally (at the request of their congregation, who wanted to keep them). Some escaped, but the one hundred twenty-nine who did not were brought to trial and were taken as slaves to the coal mines of Vorkuta. Twenty-nine of them never returned. Those who managed to return continued to practice their profession secretly, in private homes, and at great risk.

The persecution of the Roman Catholic and the Protestant churches was just as severe, only perhaps somewhat less systematic. In 1945 there were forty-five Roman Catholic priests in Subcarpathia; in 1989 there were three left. The first Roman Catholic priest was deported in 1945, fifteen more in 1948, and in later years they were also tried and sentenced to prison camp on charges of illegal religious propaganda. Almost all of the Protestant ministers were also deported after a false trial.

For a while I continued taking the children to church, and they were prepared for their First Communion. However, after I had been warned repeatedly at my work place that it was not advisable to do so, we stopped going to church, and continued to practice our religion at home. I could risk neither my job nor my children's position at school. Lia and Öcsi learned that Christmas and Easter were celebrated behind closed doors. On these holidays they did not feel like going to school at all, but I sent them because their absence would have been conspicuous. We celebrated after school. It seldom troubled them that our values were different from those respected at school. Among my colleagues I did not have to pretend at all; we were all of the same stamp.

Our cooperative, employing around five hundred people, operated successfully and kept growing. I worked there as a central cashier. All the workshops—the tailors, hatters, watchmakers, shoemakers, tile stove builders, flatiron manufacturers, and balance manufacturers—brought their daily income to me. I added up the money, entered it into the books, put it into bags, sealed the bags, and eventually handed them over to the bank couriers. The following day I received a certificate whether or not the money I sent corresponded to the account. I was in a much better situation than I used to be in my previous cashier's job: it was not my responsibility to take the money to the bank. I did not have to work overtime, unless the bank couriers were late, which meant an extra half hour at most. My work place was also close to our apartment.

It was customary that workers with a higher income rounded down the kopecks at the end of the amount of their wages. By the time I paid everybody's wages, the kopecks made up quite a nice sum; enough to buy some chocolate for the children. Nobody ever talked about this; it happened tacitly. Despite this bonus, paydays were the hardest for me. The employees of the cooperative, working all over the city, could not be gathered for meetings, so our boss held all the obligatory meetings on paydays. I was allowed to pay them only after the workers had sat through the meeting.

It was also my job to compare work sheets with reality. I did not see what went on in the workshops, but I knew that, for example, the tailors made and sold as many as three dresses with one work sheet; that was the only way for them to have some extra income. No one knew better than I how much such extra income was needed! Those people also had to get along somehow! They would have torn me apart if I had thought otherwise. We held together, and as a consequence, we worked in a good atmosphere, despite our misery. The hatters, for example, made hats as presents for every woman among us, and the tailors also sent word if some nice material arrived. In other workshops we needed no favors. For instance, we did not want a flatiron heated by coal, the type of flatiron that our cooperative manufactured! In the Soviet era we were allowed to resume correspondence with my American family—naturally, under strict control—in 1949. We received the first letter from Mommy and Daddy a few days after Sanyi's arrest. It contained photos of the family. At last I could show my children their grandparents! My sister had grown up and gotten married in the meantime. Her adult face was also new to me. Thanks to a photographer friend of Csöpike's, we, too, were able to send them photos of the children. It meant a lot to me that, though I was left alone without Sanyi, I could still get in touch with my parents again.

My asthma continued to torture me. My doctor persuaded me to undergo a minor operation, barely more than an injection, in the course of which foreign tissue from a placenta would be implanted in my body. I decided to try it. I would certainly not die from it! The tissue was implanted in a tiny incision on my back. My doctor said it would either be absorbed or rejected. It made me very sick, and I came down with a high temperature and shivered constantly. Eventually, however, the implanted tissue was absorbed, and I had no symptoms of asthma for three months! For the first time since I had gotten ill, my condition finally improved. My doctor proposed that he repeat the operation. I was afraid of getting myself into such a grave condition with such a high fever again, but eventually I underwent the operation for a second time as well. This time the implanted tissue did not get absorbed for a long time, but was not rejected either. For at least six weeks I felt some fluid moving about in my back. A nurse I knew offered to look at the wound and to try to do something about it. She mixed together some potion, and asked Csöpike to drip it onto the wound under the bandage. With the help of the pack recommended by her, the tissue was slowly absorbed, and I did not have any fits of breathlessness for half a year! My doctor was very much excited about the success, and he talked me into a third operation. I underwent the procedure for the third time as well, and I have not had any asthma symptoms ever since! My period of grave illness ended in 1952. I still do not understand what happened.

In general, we lived a quiet life. The children attended the Hungarian school, and I worked, keeping my eyes open for opportunities that might arise so as to improve our situation. We wrote letters to Sanyi, or more precisely, we had letters written to him, since people in prison camps were allowed to write and get letters only in Russian. Whenever a photo was taken of us, we asked for two copies so that we could send one of them to our daddy.

Our main goal was to fill the parcels that we were allowed to send to Sanyi every six weeks. Sanyi wrote us in every letter that we should not send him anything, but I thought he only wanted to spare us. I learned only after he had come home that every parcel put him in direct danger of losing his life. In the labor camp, too, people would kill for a good parcel. The delicacies that we obtained by our blood and sweat, he had to hand over untouched to the criminals among them. If he had not done so, he would have been killed!

The parcels consisted of things that I obtained literally at the price of my blood. Every six weeks I went to the blood bank, where, owing to my contacts, I sold 500 milliliters of blood, instead of the 300 milliliters officially allowed. My "contact" was Csöpike, who worked there. The blood bank paid 10 rubles for 100 ml blood, when 30 rubles already counted as a good monthly salary. So I was paid 50 rubles every six weeks, which was sufficient for quite a decent parcel. While we saved at home for the parcels to be sent to Sanyi, he saved whatever little he was paid for us instead of spending it in the canteen.

I filled the parcels with dry sausage, salami, bacon, and sugar. I also prepared thickening for Sanyi to cook with, and packed it in cellophane. Every prisoner had a pan, which they could also use for cooking, provided they had something to cook. A delicacy we had—which I have not seen elsewhere—was the "coffee cube" and the "cocoa cube": powdered coffee or cocoa mixed with powdered milk and sugar, pressed into a cube shape, which had to be dissolved in water before drinking. (My children actually also ate the cubes like candy.) I always put coffee and cocoa cubes as well into Sanyi's parcels.

A cousin of Sanyi's worked at the slaughterhouse. He regularly brought us the finest salami and bacon, both for Sanyi and for ourselves. It was a great help that I had something to give to the children in the mornings and in the evenings.

Many people supported us in various ways, but we received the greatest help from Csöpike and her family. Whenever we needed a doctor or had some other kind of medical problem, we turned to her. She always asked me to do my ironing at their place, allegedly because that way we entertained each other in the meantime. In fact, she wanted to reduce my electric bill.

Csöpike lived with her parents. She did not want to get married in

Uzhhorod by any means! Her sister lived in Budapest, and her dream was to get to Budapest, too, which came true later. In Uzhhorod she was surrounded by a large circle of friends, but she had closest relations with us. It meant a lot to me psychologically that she stood by us. It was due primarily to her help and to the support of other friends of ours that I never felt that the Lord had forsaken us.

Our family, on the other hand, could not be counted on, just like during the war. Sanyi, of course, did not know that. In fact, he never fully learned how nonchalantly they behaved with us during the war. I did not tell him everything because I did not want to upset him, and I did not want to create tensions in the family. I cannot stand exasperation and quarrelling. Whatever I felt towards them, I was careful to maintain normal relations with every member of the family. True, my sister-in-law and her husband did not do well in the Soviet era. Their house and store had been expropriated, and what they got for them was not enough to buy another house, so in Khust (Hungarian: Huszt) they had to build a new house mostly with their own hands. Their support was confined to sometimes inviting Lia, my sister-in-law's goddaughter, in the summer.

Otherwise, the children spent their summer holidays in pioneer camps. There were two wonderful pioneer camps half an hour away from Uzhhorod on the banks of the Uzh: one at Antalovtsi and another one at Nevyts'ke (Nevicke). These camps were ordinary holiday camps for children. The "pioneer" label did not mean that they went in for ideological education. Lia adored camp life. Some children did not like the soldierly discipline, but according to Lia, we maintained soldierlike discipline at home, too, so it was not something she had to get used to.

The campers were awakened by a bugle call at six a.m., and they began the day with wake-up exercises. The exercises were followed by washing, which my children found particularly amusing. In the yard there was a long trough, above which fifteen cans were fixed. The cans were filled with water, and if they flipped a tiny rod at their bottom, the water started running out. The cans were refilled from a bucket. When washed and dressed, the pioneers gathered around the flagpole and raised the Soviet banner. They reported to the commander of the camp and listened to the order of the day. The fixed part of the program also included a two-hour siesta, which was observed very strictly. Strangely, its Russian name was *mërtvyi chas* (the dead hour), perhaps because of the mortal silence that was forced upon the children. They finished the day with a campfire, by the light of which they hauled down the banner and evaluated the day, setting up as examples the children who performed some heroic deeds. Once it was Lia who was brought in front of the whole camp and was rewarded with the honor of lowering the flag because she saved the life of the little sister of Mari Tóth, who was drowning in the Uzh. I was very proud of her!

My children were excellent swimmers. In those years, however, they could only swim in the river Uzh. The public swimming pool in Uzhhorod had been expropriated by the sports association. From that time on, private persons were not let in.

The soldierly framework of camp life was filled with excellent programs. They went on excursions, engaged in sports, played games, visited other camps, watched theater performances, read library books and discussed them, sang in a choir, and sometimes they even performed plays themselves.

The children were looked after very conscienciously in these camps. They had three meals: cream of wheat with tea for breakfast; goulash or buckwheat broth with meat for dinner; and some biscuits or cakes for supper, unless they roasted bacon for themselves. They were given cod liver oil and orange juice twice a week. They underwent regular medical checkups. They never brought home ticks or lice or other parasites.

A while ago I showed my grandchildren the former pioneer camp. All they said was "Poor Mommy!" For us those two camps were like paradise! Lest Lia and Öcsi be bored with camping, they spent the two months of the summer holidays at two different camps. There was a direct bus line to both camp sites, so I could visit them every day. While I worked, they were on vacation, and still we did not have to be separated. What is more, because of our financial situation the first month of the camp was free of charge, and we only had to pay twenty-five percent of the regular fee for the second month, too.

As for me, my "leisure" time was still almost completely taken up by procuring the essentials. After rationing was over, commerce was liberated in principle. However, this did not mean in the least that we went into a store and bought whatever we needed. Far from it! Where rationing left off, "distribution" came in. They always distributed whatever happened to be available. Whatever was being distributed, it was worth joining the queue, because there was no knowing when that thing would be distributed again. We invariably stood in line for literally everything—for flour, sugar, butter, meat, whatever—just that after a while we queued up with kopecks instead of coupons.

The poultry butcher, for example, opened at two p.m., but distribution only began after working hours, around four or four-thirty. If we joined the line at that time, with about a thousand people before us, we were sure not to get anything. Therefore, a member of the family began to stand in the line at two, waiting for the distribution to begin. The speed of the line's progress varied. If, for example, block-butter was being distributed, which had to be cut up and weighed, the line proceeded very slowly. If, on the other hand, they distributed prepacked butter, we moved forward quickly. The children were the best at standing in line, especially Öcsi. He skilfully zigzagged among the legs of women, who overlooked his impertinence—he was such a nice little boy. The kids often managed to take their turn more than once!

The flour was distributed in six-pound sacks, and the sugar in two pounds, but if someone lined up twice, he could get two portions. In the preserves season we needed much more sugar than two pounds, so every available member of the family had to stand in line. Sometimes the children maneuvered so skilfully that they got the necessary amount before my turn came, so we could all go home early.

We spent half of our lives standing in line. What was worse, people could not behave in these situations in a civilized way. Often huge rows arose, and even the most peaceful lines broke up before the door, and the happy ending was invariably spoiled by nasty jostling and elbowing. I could never understand why people made life, which was not easy anyway, even harder for themselves.

In the line it was impossible to read because of those who were trying to be smart, and because of the fact that the line was basically continuously in motion. We spent the time talking and exchanging recipes. In summer we would sweat in the sun, in winter we nearly froze in the snow, and we had to stand there for hours even when we were sick since life had to go on. This whole system was devised well. It took up all our time. People who must spend every minute they have procuring goods are not engaged in anything else. And those who do not think do not create any problems.

The stocks we "piled up" as a result of these distributions were stored in a pit dug in our garden. Everything required a different storing method. For example, the butter, of which we received 400 grams (nearly a pound) at a time, had to be kept underwater in the pit; that way it did not grow rancid. We could keep all kinds of food for quite a long time. We obtained a refrigerator only in 1963.

My life was made significantly easier by an excellent self-service laundry. It opened with three washing machines, then it expanded, and eventually it had eight washing machines, as well as some spin driers, driers, and flatirons. I would arrive with a large pile of laundry, and in two to three hours I could take home clothes ready to be put into the wardrobe. We still had no bathroom at home. We brought in water from the well in the yard, washed in a washbowl, and used an outhouse, so the laundromat was a real luxury for us. I loved going there.

The year 1952 brought a change in our lives because the first parcels from America arrived. What is more, four parcels all at once! It was a real sensation! They contained bed linen, towels, dresses, underwear, shoes—everything we needed. At last I could also present Csöpike with a few nice things in return for all the good things she did for us. The items that we could do without were sold, and the money we got for them also came in useful.

I have always adored beautiful things. I had been longing to be dressed nicely, and at last this desire of mine was fulfilled. The children were also dressed wonderfully from head to toe. Little Lia gladly put on the leather coat, the lined raincoat, the trousers, or the shoes she received, but she did not want to wear the nice little American dresses. She did not like dressing up, perhaps because earlier she did not have the opportunity to get to like it. Besides, she did not want to be different from all the other children who were dressed just as miserably as we had been before the arrival of the parcels. Later Lia, too, realized that there was nothing wrong with putting on a nice piqué dress. Owing to the parcels, from that time on we dressed beautifully even amidst the greatest poverty.

Since the American presents were practically all we had, we regretted very much that the customs officers opened the parcels brutally, with a blade, always damaging the things on top. They often also pilfered from the parcels, as was clear from the list attached.

After the parcels began coming from America, we did not really need Aunt Olga's dinners any more. Mommy found out that we did not actually receive as much as they sent to Aunt Olga's daughter in Budapest. Furthermore, at that time I already had a job with normal working hours and I was even healthy again, so I could resume cooking myself. Therefore, Mommy decided that they would support us directly in the form of parcels. As the central cashier of our cooperative, I had to go to the bank every day. I timed my visits to the bank so they were right after lunch. This way I could extend my lunchtime a little bit. I would wait at home for the children to arrive from school, and we had lunch together like a proper family. More precisely, like a proper family without a father.

We also shared experiences other than having lunch and standing in line; for example, the American, Indian, or old Hungarian films that we saw in the Uzhhorod cinema. We also regularly went to symphony concerts and to the performances that the Berehovo theater company held in the Uzhhorod theater. In certain periods there were also guest performances by companies from Hungary which we enjoyed very much.

In 1953, after the seventh grade, Lia sat for an entrance examination at the Uzhhorod high school of fine arts. She obtained outstanding results. The artist examiners all congratulated us on Lia's great talent. They said that someone who could draw such an excellent portrait without any preliminary training must study art by all means. She was admitted, and knowing that, we spent the summer holidays in high spirits. By the time the school year began, however, her name had been crossed off the list of the students admitted. Of all the decisions and measures discriminating against our children because of their father's fate, this was the most painful one. Lia did not try to get into the art school again. She was deeply hurt, and decided she would go away from here at the first chance. She had no definite plans, but she was sure she wanted to leave Uzhhorod and she wanted to leave the country.

For the time being, nevertheless, we had to find a school for Lia in Uzhhorod. As the Hungarian school ended with the seventh grade, I was compelled to enroll her in a Russian school. I hired a student to teach her Russian. Lia learned quickly, she understood everything, but even so the Russian school was too exhausting for her. One day she collapsed at school and was sent home. The doctor diagnosed some heart disorder. I could not believe it. I found it absurd that such a tireless child, an outstanding athlete, should have a heart disease, so I took her to the best specialist. His diagnosis was the same! He recommended that she be removed from school and be kept at home to rest. That was what I did. During the day she usually stayed at Csöpike's place with Csöpike's mother, or she went over to Mamuka's. In the afternoons we took a walk that was not strenuous for her on our street. I tried to strengthen her, but her health did not improve.

She was also hospitalized for a while. In the Soviet Union there was

practically no medicine, and so her heart disease was treated with paraffin, salicyl, and cognac. No wonder the poor child's condition got
even worse. A nurse suggested to us that if we really had American
relatives we should ask them for medicine. I made quick arrangements,
and by means of the Red Cross we soon received a medicine called
terramycin from America. Lia reacted to it very well and she recovered
quickly. When she did not need anything anymore but injections, she
was released to come home. The injections were given to her by Csöpike,
who administered them best at the blood bank.

Eventually we found out what caused Lia's heart problems. At the
age of four she had her tonsils removed. A stump which was left behind or grew back suppurated, and now it had to be removed before it
had fatal consequences. Poor Lia bore the operation quite patiently.
Then she got the measles, after which her heart complaints briefly re-
sumed. She was sent to a sanatorium and there she fully recovered at
last. Her illness took up basically the whole school year.

Lia's disease had another reason, too, besides the suppurated stump.
At the Russian school she was called upon to join the Komsomol. It
was a privilege to be admitted to the "vanguard"! Those who aspired to
be members had to study hard and had to be of impeccable character,
blameless in every respect. Lia did not want to become a member of the
Komsomol, by any means! She ceased studying. She made a public
statement that her father had been sentenced unjustly and had been
taken to the taiga as a slave, and she could only bear this unjustice done
to our family because she believed in the help of God. My quiet, with-
drawn little girl brought herself to this because she wanted to dissuade
the Komsomol from wanting her. It did not help, though! Lia was such
a good athlete, and the Komsomol organization of her school wanted to
increase their glory with her successes so much, that she was admitted
despite everything. There was no way to avoid it. At the ceremony
when the new Komsomol members took the oath, Lia did not say the
words but merely murmured because she did not want to commit perjury.

Lia was very much distressed by her Komsomol membership. Not
wanting to attract any attention in Uzhhorod, she took a train to the
most distant Hungarian city of Subcarpathia, Khust, with two friends
of hers, to confess the sin of having joined the Komsomol. The priest
of Khust did not make things easier for Lia. He ranted at the poor child
that she had sold her soul to the devil, for which there was no absolution! Lia told him that she did everything to avoid sinning; she openly

confessed her faith. She also explained what situation our family was in, but the priest did not relent. The poor child almost broke down! After a long period of bargaining, the priest absolved Lia under the condition that the absolution would only be effective if she never again did anything in the Komsomol. Lia was glad to be absolved, but she was worried about how she could satisfy the condition. From the drawing circle to the sports circle, all her activities took place under the auspices of the Komsomol. How could she remain completely passive? She returned to school preoccupied with trying to find a solution. It was on that day that she collapsed and became ill! As a consequence of her illness, she quit the Russian school, and together with the school, she quit the Komsomol for good. So my little Lia regarded her disease as a manifestation of God's grace. After she had recovered, I was willing to believe her.

While Lia was ill, Öcsi finished the seventh grade, and from the following year, the Hungarian school also opened eighth, ninth, and tenth grades, so both of them could go on studying in their own school—in Hungarian! They were in the same class. They studied together, they did their homework together, and they stuck together in everything else, too; they were very close to each other. One of their cousins, Éva Laszota, was also in the same class, so in that class three Laszotas passed their final exams in 1957.

The American medicine that cured Lia had a long story still. The six-month-old daughter of my friend, Aliz Teke, fell ill with cerebral meningitis. That disease was rather common in this area. Two of Lia's fourteen-year-old classmates died of it. Ottilia, the little girl, was in a frightful condition at the Mukachevo hospital. She did not react to anything. Aliz did not move from her daughter's bedside, while her husband, Sándor Kaluja, commuted between the hospital and us. In despair, he brought us worse and worse news. Then it occurred to Csöpike's father that the description of the medicine sent for Lia said that it was also good for meningitis. I looked for it immediately. The instructions said that for infants one third of a capsule had to be dissolved in milk. Ottilia's father rushed with the medicine to Mukachevo. He got there late in the evening. The doctors did not want to give it to the little girl because they did not know what it was. Poor Ottilia already lay stiff. The head physician of the hospital eventually decided that the child had only a few hours left, so she would certainly not be killed by the strange medicine; therefore, he allowed Aliz to give it to her. Aliz forced her mouth open, and dripped the milky solution into it. Towards dawn Ottilia's eyes stirred, and after the second dose she woke up. Her condition kept improving rapidly, and two months later her mother took her home completely healthy. The news about the wonder medicine, which cured both Lia and Ottilia, spread all over the city.

Christmas and Easter were not only workdays. The longest meetings were also always timed to fall on these holidays. On one Christmas Day I was away again participating in some meeting, and Lia and Öcsi were decorating the tree, when a strange woman rushed into our apartment, looking for me. When she learned that I was not at home, she asked the children where we kept the medicines. They gave her the box. She snatched the American medicine out of it, threw in a handful of money, and ran off. When I got home, the children could not even tell me who had been to our place. However, the money she left in the box was more than a year's salary for me. A few weeks later the woman returned and gave me back whatever was left of the terramycin. She told me that her husband had been about to die of meningitis. He was unconscious when she gave him the first dose of terramycin on an airplane heading for Kiev. When they got to the Kiev hospital, the doctor declared it had been unnecessary to fly him to Kiev because he was already in a satisfactory condition. That man also fully recovered, and the rest of the medicine cured two more people still!

CHAPTER 19

The vast taiga had prison camps scattered on it. Areas of twenty-five hectares (about sixty acres) were selected for deforestation. They were enclosed, a watchtower was erected at each of their four corners for guards with submachine guns, and a prison camp was organized on each of them. The one where Sanyi was kept was inhabited by two thousand prisoners.

When Sanyi and his fellow prisoners arrived at the camp, they were divided into barracks, they listened to the daily program, they were given their clothes: a shirt, a pair of trousers, a cap, a pair of gloves, footcloths, overgarments for summer and winter, and shoes, and they began work right away. From the second day on, they got up around three to four in the morning every day. Nobody had a watch, so they never knew exactly what time it was. The prisoners each received 2 liters (3.5 pints) of water for washing themselves, as well as two dishes, a smaller one and a bigger one. They washed by slowly pouring the water from the smaller dish, while catching it in the larger one so that it could still be used. Once in every ten days they could wash themselves more thoroughly; it was called "the bath."

After washing they went to the dining hall, where the work groups—the so-called brigades—got breakfast in turns. They had to pass in front of three windows. At the first window they were allotted their bread ration for the whole day: 800 grams (somewhat less then two pounds) of brown bread, as well as a ladle of hot soup made of cabbage, cucumber, or both. At the second window they were given a ladle of gruel, and at the third window two thimblefuls of oil on the gruel. Considering the hard work they were to do during the day, this amount was barely enough to keep them going. After breakfast they left the aluminum bowls they ate from on the tables; the dishes were washed by other prisoners. The cleaning and the cooking took place in the dining hall. According to Sanyi the kitchen area, the dining hall, and the dishes were all kept very clean. Efforts were made to prevent epidemics. Then the prisoners left for work. They walked two and a half miles on average to the lumbering site, they worked there so hard that they were running with sweat in summer and winter alike, then they walked two and a half miles again back to the barracks. In summer they worked in linen clothes and in rubber-soled shoes. For the winter they received quilted trousers, a *pufaika* (a short quilted jacket), a *bushlat* (a long quilted coat to be worn over the *pufaika*), a quilted cap, quilted gloves, quilted socks, and *valenki*, i.e., wadded felt-boots. Naturally, packed in so much wadding, it was hard to move. Those who were afraid of the cold put on everything, but Sanyi did not need the *bushlat* even when the temperature was below -30° centigrade (-25° Fahrenheit); he always went working wearing only his *pufaika*. In the prison camp everyone had his own nail in the wall. Sanyi hung his *bushlat* on his nail the very first day, and it remained there for the rest of the years.

They proceeded to the working area with an armed guard before them and another behind them, as if there was some place for them to escape to. But there was not; all they could see was the boundless taiga and boundless snow, or in the spring, when the snow was melting, boundless water and mud. At the gate of the camp they were counted by the guards and were supplied with instruments: saws, drills, and axes.

Work began as soon as they got to the lumbering site. They worked for about nine hours a day until dark. In fact, it never really became dark there. In the summer the nights were light because the sun barely set below the horizon, and in the winter, because the snow reflected light. Sanyi said they had so much snow that even the path on which they trod hard was covered by a meter of snow!

In principle, they should have received hot lunch at the work site, but the commander did not have their lunch taken there. It was simpler to let them take along part of their bread ration which they ate in the brief break at noon. When eating and smoking, they took off their gloves, and still their hands did not freeze. Sanyi says that if one's hands are very cold, one has to rub them with snow and must make them work hard, and then they do not get frozen even in -40° centigrade.

Sanyi's brigade consisted of thirty-five men. Their foreman, who taught them everything, was a young Russian. He was sentenced to seven years for killing a civilian in Germany during the war when he was a soldier. He liked Sanyi, perhaps because Sanyi could speak Russian, or because he always gave him salami, bacon, and sugar from the parcels that I sent him. The foreman often told Sanyi that he should not worry because he was under his protection. They did need protection, because the political prisoners were kept together with the most unscrupulous criminals. These criminals, the so-called *blatnye*, killed for anything. They usually kept away from my husband, because the foreman could have them killed if they harassed a person under his protection, but even so they robbed Sanyi twice. In the parcels that I sent to Sanyi I sometimes also hid some money in addition to the delicacies and the thirty packages of "Verhovina" brand cigarettes, so that he could buy himself things in the canteen. The criminals once robbed him of twenty-five rubles, and another time, of fifty rubles, which were huge sums of money!

Once I put a fifty-ruble bill in a parcel sent to Sanyi. I thought one bill was easier to hide. One evening my husband went over to the canteen with his money to buy 100 grams of jam to eat with his brown bread. The canteen keeper told him it was not a good idea, that jam could not be so important!—but in vain. My poor Sanyi did not understand what he meant! He realized only afterwards that the canteen keeper wanted to warn him, because he saw that two criminals were watching Sanyi. Since he could not talk Sanyi out of the jam, he weighed him 100 grams of it, and gave him back forty-nine rubles. Sanyi started off for his barracks with the jam and the money in his hands, and as soon as he stepped out of the building, he was attacked by two young criminals. One of them squeezed his throat, while the other one wrested the money out of his hand. Poor Sanyi was throttled so hard that he could not speak for two weeks. It was a miracle that he survived the incident! I am afraid it was the most expensive jam of his life.

In the canteen they could buy slices of bread, biscuits, and sweets. The prisoners worked for fixed wages, but most of the money they earned was deducted to cover their room and board. There was barely anything left for them to spend in the canteen, and Sanyi saved even that little money and sent it to us! We received fifty rubles twice or three times through postal transfer.

Returning to the prisoners' daily work, they had to cut down lumber and build a road using the wood on the precipice. It was the length of the road to be completed every day that was prescribed for them. The road had to be 2.5 meters (about 8.5 feet) wide, but they had to clear a 3-meter (10 feet) wide lane for it. The forest was made up of birch, poplar, and pine trees. They had to cut the trunks at 10 centimeters above the ground, which meant that in winter they had to brush away the snow first. Then they had to dig out the roots, no matter how frozen hard the soil was. Birch roots were the hardest to dig out, for they went down very deep. They had to do a perfect job because a single root left in tore up the finished road when it began to sink. If they did not carry out every phase of the job perfectly, they had to start it all over again.

Where the soil was marshy, the road required special foundations. They wove a net out of young pines and lay it on the marshy soil under the road. They covered the net with huge logs, across which they placed ties. The ties, however, were not simply put on top of the logs, but they were jointed to them one by one. Then the ties jointed to the logs were covered by a thick wooden floor. Finally, they built a strong wooden curb on both sides of the road. The new road was used by eight- to ten-ton trucks packed with lumber. If a truck had slid off the road or had turned over, there would have been no way to set it right again. So that a wheel hitting against the curb could not push it off, they drilled holes into it, and fastened it with wedges, which were held by wooden nails.

My Sanyi did this work for five years with no day off. Actually, they could have got a day off every month, but it turned out at the beginning that after toiling for thirty days, it is impossible to stop for a day. On that day they all felt very sick, they ached in every limb. Knowing that, they did not use up even that single day per month.

The labor process began with the first swing of an axe in a virgin area and ended with the acceptance of the finished, impeccable road. In the first days the foreman showed them the technique and the tricks, and set the thirty-five persons the norm of four meters of road per day. Many of them, however, could not endure that. After six weeks there were only twenty-eight persons left. The foreman, nevertheless, found that they had already acquired the knack of it, and raised the norm to eight meters per day—for the twenty-eight of them! "The state cannot keep you for free!" he kept saying, as if they had wanted to be kept by the state! By the time they could fulfil the norm of eight meters per day, only twenty-four of them remained. Then the norm was raised to twelve meters a day. Eventually, only sixteen of them were left. The sixteen of them could stand everything: the cold, the food, the work, and even the ever raised norms. They were divided into four groups of four persons, and each group had to build a six-meter road every day. They organized their work perfectly. They distributed the different jobs among themselves in such a way that each person was doing what he was best at. They were driven mercilessly, like slaves! The road they built served the purpose of forwarding lumber from the taiga to the railway, and through the railway, to all parts of the country, some of which were still in ruins as a consequence of the war.

What moved me most in Sanyi's account was that he was able to like his work also under those inhumane conditions. It seems that in order to preserve his dignity, a man wants to see his activity in all circumstances as one with a purpose, and he finds satisfaction in his work if he feels he has created something to further that purpose. Sanyi was proud if he saw heavy trucks packed with lumber riding on his road, and the road did not as much as give a crack. Actually, if it did (because they could not really see what the soil was like deeply below it) they immediately repaired it, wedging it where it was necessary.

Not only were the roads strange in the taiga but the vehicles, as well. The large trucks capable of carrying a load of six to ten tons were driven by gas, instead of gasoline, and the gas was produced from birch billets by a power gas generator.

After work, in the evening, the brigade marched back to the camp. They took off their wet clothes, washed, and went to the dining hall. They were given lunch and dinner at the same time. They received hot soup, two portions of gruel, and four thimblefuls of oil. They also received a finger-seized piece of fish and a spoonful of sugar. They could have as much tea as they wanted, but they also prepared another kind of drink for themselves. They soaked left-over pieces of bread in water and let it ferment. The resulting sourish drink could apparently taste good during day-long lumbering.

The "bath" on every tenth day took place as follows. Everyone got a wash bowl, which was half-filled with water heated in cauldrons by the bath attendant. The attendant also gave each of them a piece of soap the size of a fingernail. That was the equipment they had to bathe with from top to toe. If the bath attendant was in a good mood, then after they had poured out the dirty water, he gave them an additional half a bowl of clean water as well. "Bathing" was followed by shaving. Once every ten days they were shaved on the head, on the cheeks, and all over—without any soap.

Their commander was very particular about cleanliness. Once someone brought in body lice from the outside. They immediately collected everybody's clothes and disinfected them in hot steam. Actually, the clothes were disinfected practically every day. Despite the cold weather, the prisoners lumbering for the whole day sweated heavily. In the evening everything they had on, from the underwear to the quilted jacket, was wet. When they got home, they took off everything, including their shoes, and put them on an iron ring. These rings were collected by other prisoners, and were taken to the drying room. In the course of drying the clothes were also disinfected. They got back their clothes in the morning before leaving for work. The rings with the dry clothes were hanging on a long bar. As Sanyi said, everybody immediately recognized his own clothes, even though they all looked alike. As a result of these measures, there were no lice and no bedbugs in the camp, and no major epidemic occurred, either.

Every labor camp had a hospital barrack, led by a surgeon. Naturally, the surgeon was also one of the prisoners. The hospital barrack of Sanyi's camp did not deserve that name at all, as there was practically no medical equipment in it. Prisoners were vaccinated against typhus and some other diseases once a year. The vaccination took place as follows: the prisoners were lined up with their trousers pulled down, and the surgeon injected each of them with ten milliliters of vaccine— each of them with the same syringe; the only syringe of the hospital barrack. It was never even wiped since there was no alcohol to wipe it with. Luckily Sanyi asked not to be vaccinated and he never became ill. He had to go to the hospital only once, because of an accident.

Next to the road proper, they also built smaller ways for wheelbarrows: for hand-barrows pushed by prisoners, and for larger wheelbarrows drawn by horses. One morning, Sanyi slid on such a boardway while pushing a barrow, and an axe cut into his foot. The wound opened like a rose, but it did not bleed. The medical assistant sprinkled it with some powder, but he put no bandage on it. Sanyi sat with an open wound until the end of the workday, when with the help of the others he hopped on one foot into the camp. For at least half of the way, the others carried him on their arms after a day's work. Political prisoners stuck together unbelievably. They helped each other in every possible way, even though they were of different nationalities: Ukrainians, Hungarians, Georgians, Latvians, Lithuanians, Russians, etc.

When the surgeon caught sight of Sanyi's foot, he started lamenting: he said it had already mortified. Nevertheless, he attended to the wound, he cleaned it, put ointment on it, and joined it with seven clips. "You will have a rest here," he said, and, indeed, he kept Sanyi in the hospital for three weeks. Sanyi spent the time reading the Russian books of the camp's library. The surgeon saved Sanyi's foot, even if it hurt, and still hurts, very much.

Another time Sanyi had a terrible toothache. The surgeon disinfected the only pliers of the camp in flames, and attacked the huge molar. After struggling for an hour and a half, he tore out half of it, leaving the other half for the following day, lest the great massacre have fatal consequences. Some pieces of the tooth must have been left in, however, since that place still hurts if Sanyi bites on it. The six-year "camping" cost Sanyi all his teeth. He came home with five teeth, which had to be pulled out here in Uzhhorod. Fortunately, in other respects he remained healthy.

In the evening, when the sky was clear, Sanyi looked for the Great Bear, the Little Bear, and the Pole Star. They seemed to be so close, almost within reach. He looked for the direction of Uzhhorod, and asked of the sky what his wife and two small children could be doing two thousand kilometers away. He did not know if we were left alone by the authorities or were also persecuted. Little Lia often asked her daddy to let her sit on his bike, but daddy was always in a hurry, or just he thought it was dangerous, in any case, they did not bike together. Sanyi had qualms every day that he did not do even that for his dear little daughter, and he would not be able to do it for her any more.

Though each prisoner knew that they were taken to the taiga for good, they were hoping against hope. Hope is a great force; it sustains people also in the most desperate situations. Some people hoped that the Americans would help if they found out what was going on there. Sanyi tried to wake them up: the Americans knew very well whom they took up with when they made an alliance against Hitler with Stalin. Others were waiting for Stalin to die. They hoped that then things would take a turn. Many prisoners were hoping for a miracle.

The prison camp was, in fact, ruled by the most ruthless criminals. They kept killing unscrupulously and usually went unpunished. They were constantly making bets, and those who lost and could not pay were stabbed to death. On the night of Stalin's death there was a great showdown among them; they killed twenty-nine men in one night. They lay the twenty-nine corpses in line in front of the guards' room. In the morning, when the guards saw what had happened, they ordered the twenty-nine corpses to be buried, and the case was never mentioned again. No one was made responsible for it.

Once Sanyi was called in by the political officer and was shown three photos. He should have recognized some Ukrainian nationalists in the pictures. He did not recognize them, even after the officer threatened him with a transfer to an even stricter prison camp. After Sanyi came out of his office, the camp criminals surrounded him and warned him that stool pigeons were punished with death. Sanyi explained to them that he did not go there on his own—he was ordered to go there. He could barely convince them that he did not denounce anyone. When they let him go eventually, they told him they would keep an eye on him.

Sanyi was able to endure the cold, the hard work, even the harassing of criminals. What he found unbearable was the insect attacks in the summer. He says we cannot imagine the invasion of mosquitoes that they experienced. The mosquitoes made the sky grow dark! The bites of the huge yellow horseflies grew into flaming swellings. The only comfort of prisoners was revenge. If they could catch a yellow horsefly, they pushed a straw into its behind and enjoyed seeing how it struggled for a while after taking off and then fell down buzzing. The little grey gadflies slipped in everywhere; they found the smallest openings in the prisoners' clothes and bit their bodies—and the prisoners could not take revenge for this! People waited throughout the summer for the first frost to arrive, since from then on they did not have to suffer from insects any longer.

The barracks were built from round logs carefully fit together at the corners. The tiny rifts among the logs were filled by moss. Houses built with that technology kept the heat very well. If they were heated properly, they were really warm. So after work, the detainees could rest in a pleasant temperature. They were too tired to do anything, except perhaps to play games. They regularly played chess, checkers, and morris. They drew the board and sculpted the figures from bread. The black chessmen were smeared with soot.

Every prisoner was allowed to write to his family once a month in Russian and under strict censorship. Every postcard said the same: "How are you? I am well. Take care of yourselves!" My letters were translated into Russian by my friend Aliz. This kind of correspondence only served the purpose of letting each other know that the other was still alive. However, I also learned the truth about Sanyi from letters sent illegally: what he did, what he ate, how they were treated, how they actually lived. I did not understand what was going on when I received the first letter of that kind. Sanyi described everything, and I was terrified that he would be killed for it. I realized only later that the first real letter was not sent via the camp post.

I received at least twice as many illegally sent letters as official ones. As I found out later, the illegal correspondence was carried out in the following way. The brigades of nonpolitical offenders were allowed to move freely both in the camp and in the working area. The guards knew them, and did not search them at the gate. These prisoners were the mailmen; it was to them that everybody gave his letters. Sometimes they carried as many as one hundred letters hidden under their clothes. Before loading the wagons with lumber, they hid the letters under birchbark. These wagons got to all parts of the country, and that was why I once received mail from Sverdlovsk, then from Odessa, or Kazan'. The wagons arrived at sawmills where the workers were also prisoners. When unloading the wagons, they had to sweep them clean, so every letter was found. They handed them over to their colleagues moving about freely, who put them in the regular mail. Masses of people not knowing each other were cooperating. The operation of the illegal mail was an example of the solidarity of simple people. In fact, it was more than that. It was an example of a silent, nationwide resistance to Stalin's terror. Unknown people participated in the postal chain, each of who risked his own life. Still, every illegally sent letter from Sanyi arrived. Every one of them!

Very many people did not survive the prison camps. Lots of people were killed when they were rioting. Others died of diseases or exhaustion. Sanyi is convinced that he was able to endure the ordeals owing to the spartan education he was subjected to in his parents' house. The strict upbringing had taught him patience and self-discipline, and made him a physically trained, hardened boy and young man. At home, they ate meat only twice a week. On Sundays, they had a festive dinner with fried or roasted chicken or pork, and on Thursdays they had some simpler meat-dish: goulash or hamburger. On the other days, they ate vegetables: beans, potatoes, spinach, all kinds of nutritious dishes full of vitamins. Sanyi believes it was that well-balanced diet that made him so tough. What also helped Sanyi endure was that he could not really believe that his twenty-five-year sentence would, indeed, mean twenty-five years.

Stalin's death raised great hopes in everybody. Actually, it did not bring an immediate change in everyday life. People had become much too broken, too introverted. In Stalin's time, people could be sentenced to ten years in prison camp just for telling a joke. Although the fear and anxiety was eased, we still did not feel like telling jokes. People kept quiet and spent all their time working and procuring. We stood in line before work and after work every day, just to subsist. When Stalin died, we nevertheless livened up a little bit and started believing that our daddy might come home!

It was 1953. Sanyi and his fellow prisoners also heard the news of Stalin's death. What they heard precisely was that "the rotten pig is dead." Allegedly nobody had to ask who it was. After a while the political officer summoned together the prisoners, calling them by their names for the first time, and told them that those whose hands had not been stained with blood would soon be allowed to go home. The news also spread at home that it was possible to apply for the release of political prisoners. I heard from acquaintances that they had already submitted their applications, so I also asked a lawyer I knew to formulate one for us.

I will never forget that we were just about to leave for church on Whitsun Sunday when the postman called at me, telling me that I had two letters. One came from Mommy and the other one from the prison authorities of Sanyi's camp. They informed me that they had received my application and they would reexamine Sanyi's case. At the same time the state security office at Uzhhorod also began revising its former procedures. They looked up every prisoner sentenced by them in the prison camps. By the time our application got to Sanyi's camp, the Uzhhorod authorities had already contacted him. It was already 1954, and I received more and more illegally sent letters from him. His letters sounded more and more hopeful. He felt his chances were improving. Then we were informed that Sanyi's case had been reexamined, and they would let us know the outcome. Then there came no news for a long time. The prisoners had been interrogated again, new judgments had been passed, but the authorities still did not condescend to inform the families.

The authorities also took their time before releasing their victims. Sanyi and some of his fellow prisoners were transferred to a camp called Eltsevo, which was also in the taiga, but which was crossed by the Murmansk-Arkhangelsk-Moscow railway line. There they worked in warehouses, arranging and keeping account of shoes, boots, and quilted jackets. They also had to unload potatoes and onions from wagons into clamps. After five years of lumbering, the lifting and carrying of 100-kilogram (220-pound) potato sacks was nothing for Sanyi. A forty-three-year-old man hardened by work of that kind can be very strong!

On April 18th Sanyi was summoned by the liaison officer who said to him: "Mister, you are free. You must hand in everything by four o'clock. After four you are not allowed to stay on the camp site." Well, he was not granted amnesty. They did not go that far! As a result of the reexamination, the sentence of every innocent prisoner tried was shortened exactly to the time he had spent in prison. So they were set free, but they had a criminal record.

And we still knew nothing. We were still not informed of anything!

Sanyi received his wages for six years, from which the costs of his sustenance had been deducted. He was given six hundred fifty-eight rubles, plus allowance for three days, and a railway ticket to Uzhhorod. With the money and the ticket in his pocket, he was put outside the gate. He could have gotten a new passport in a town forty kilometers (twenty-five miles) away, but he did not want to make a detour; he hurried home.

He first took a train to a city two hundred kilometers away from Eltsevo. Then he travelled another six hundred kilometers to Moscow, to the Kiev Railway Station. There he had to have his ticket and his papers stamped. When the cashier realized that he had just been released from a prison camp, she shut the window in front of him. Sanyi did not know what to do. He was not allowed to stay in Moscow for more than twenty-four hours, and his train was just about to leave. He explained to a policeman what had happened despite the fact that he had a proper certificate of discharge. The policeman ordered the cashier to stamp Sanyi's papers, so he could still jump on the train leaving for L'viv in the last minute. It was only in L'viv that he dared to send me a telegram, saying that he would arrive at eight a.m. the following day. I learned from that telegram that our ordeal was over.

CHAPTER 20

Sanyi was released from the prison camp on April 18, 1955. He arrived in Uzhhorod at eight a.m., April 22nd in his prison garb, wearing a short quilted jacket. How many of us showed up at the railway station to meet him! It was a whole delegation: family, friends, his former colleagues, as well as mine. None of us went to stand in lines that day! His parents were waiting for him at home because Mamuka was preparing the dinner. Csöpike was the first to fall on Sanyi's neck because she was standing at the door where Sanyi got off. Everybody was calling at me: "Come here! Come here!" but I was just standing transfixed. Eventually we embraced and did not want to let each other go any more!

Sanyi looked surprisingly good. Prisoners were fattened up by a special diet before being released, but Sanyi said he had been in the same condition all the time. Only that charming smile of his had disappeared! It was his facial expression in addition to his prison clothes that indicated where he had come from. Although we had sold all of Sanyi's clothes in our times of need, his clothing problems were soon solved. He got a green jacket from Csöpike's father, and others gave him shirts, trousers, shoes, underwear, so the next day he could already dress in civilian clothes.

Sanyi was particularly happy to see his children. He left them as small kids, and now they were about to finish secondary school. Although the children were in principle glad to get back their father, in practice they were jealous. Sanyi was practically an alien to them, and they were offended by the fact that from that time on they had to share me with him. After six years it took them a while to get used to having a father in the family. Apart from those initial difficulties, Sanyi fit back in the family smoothly. We have been living together in great affection and harmony ever since. We have respected each other's peace. To this very day we have never ever quarrelled!

Sanyi's attempt to find his place again took a tragicomic turn at the Uzhhorod police. He went to the police to be registered as was required, but they refused to register him in Uzhhorod and told him to go to the to the rural district (*raion*). Poor Sanyi asked in despair why he should go to the countryside when his family, his apartment, his father, his mother, and the graves of his ancestors were all in Uzhhorod. He was born in Uzhhorod just like his parents, he grew up there, so why should he go elsewhere? He also had a written permit allowing him to return to his home. The policemen had no answer, but they did not register him in Uzhhorod all the same. "OK," said Sanyi, "then I will go home without being registered. Without being registered I will have no passport, and without a passport I will have no work and no income, so I will provide for my family by stealing and robbing, and the Uzhhorod police will be to blame for that."

The following day he was called to the police with his letter of discharge, and he was registered and was given an Uzhhorod passport. He only realized at home that it said "filled on the basis of a letter of discharge." We knew that with a passport saying that he had been a prisoner he would not be able to find a job. So he rushed back to the police and objected desperately. Three days later he was called in again, and this time he got a passport which said "filled on the basis of a previous passport."

The authorities harassed Sanyi for months still, trying to persuade him to become an informer. They promised him everything, among other things a good job with a lot of money and the repeal of his criminal record. When they realized they could not convince him by any means, they left him alone.

As soon as Sanyi had decent clothes and a proper ID, he began to look for work. We all tried to help him, but it was not easy to find a job for a person who had just come home from a prison camp. Eventually he found something towards the end of the summer which I did not mind at all because he needed that much rest after all those years of hard forced labor.

Sanyi took refuge at the cooperative where I worked. Our dear director, who used to employ prisoners' wives, now employed more and more of the husbands returning from the Gulag as well, so our selected team came to represent even higher standards. Sanyi first manufactured bitumen, but it was harmful to his health. Then he polished cement plates, first by hand, later with the help of a machine. Then he became assistant to a mason building the county library.

In the meantime news got around that Sanyi was back and was looking for a proper job. The brother-in-law of a friend of mine, who was the head manager of a company, found him a job in the office of a cartwright's workshop. Sanyi became a cost accountant, so at last he could do what he was competent doing.

Although in the end Sanyi had the right papers, his former self-confidence did not return. He remained shy and distrustful. We did not speak openly about what had happened. Our acquaintances were wary of Sanyi, and he was also afraid of them. There was no knowing who was being watched and who was not, who was an informer and who was not. But what we knew the least about was what counted as a crime! We kept in touch with only three or four families. Sanyi had been vilified innocently. No wonder he wanted to keep a distance from everybody and everything. He who has been bitten by a viper will also avoid the grass snake.

Sanyi's acquaintances of the same fate were also coming home from the Gulag. When they met in the street, they were glad to see each other and to learn that the other had also survived it, but they did not speak about the Gulag among themselves, either!

It was a long time before my poor Sanyi's shyness and misanthropy was eased. First we visited Csöpike and her family together, then he also let me take him to Kati and Manyika Magyar's place. Slowly he made friends again with the Hungarian families whom we used to keep company with in the old days and who remained close to me during my years of solitude as well. Sanyi used to be very popular in our little social circle, and so he was received with exceptionally great affection. After a while we could also take him for a walk or on an excursion. Slowly his interest in fishing also returned. Once I asked a friend of ours, a doctor, to come and visit us, and at the same time also to give Sanyi a check-up. Fortunately, he found everything in order.

Sanyi loved working in the cartwright's workshop. Soon, however, all the workshops of his company doing woodwork joined together, and he was promoted to manager. On the one hand, Sanyi found his new position satisfying and adequate to his qualifications; at the same time, however, he also felt it to be a burden for several reasons. First of all, he had to work in three shifts, which disturbed our regular way of living. Besides, many people in this part of the world did not like to work at all, which Sanyi could not bear. He did not tolerate stealing, either. He would never take home as much as a mote without having paid for it. The people around him, on the other hand, would also take home the beam if they could. Sanyi's strictness in these matters was a permanent source of conflicts. So eventually he asked to be demoted to his former position in the cartwright's workshop.

Everyday life became slightly more bearable in certain respects. For example, we could obtain news from Hungary. Sanyi did not wish to listen to Radio Free Europe, but we could listen to the Budapest radio stations. It became possible to subscribe to Hungarian newspapers as well (unlike before, and unlike today), and we subscribed to two Hungarian dailies and two Hungarian magazines.

People could dress better. Ready-made clothes were still ugly beyond words, but it was not a luxury to have clothes made to order. Some of the former excellent Uzhhorod tailors were still around, and now we could also buy fairly good materials. A relatively pleasant shampoo appeared in the stores, and good-quality Polish cosmetics were also available. There was a single brand of scents: *Krasnaia Moskva* (Red Moscow), a perfume and scented soap. Every woman was reeking of it. Its pungent smell is simply indescribable. I discovered, however, an unscented baby soap, and it was that soap that we used both for washing ourselves and for washing clothes. When the border to Hungary opened a little, wonderful Hungarian cosmetics also appeared.

When Sanyi came home on April 22nd, his father had already been very sick in his lungs. He died on May 18, 1955. He waited for his son to come home, and he departed only afterwards. The lovely hearse of Uzhhorod was not in use any more. We had to take his coffin up to the Way of the Cross with a truck. The family had a little chapel with a crypt up there, and my father-in-law also wanted to rest there among his ancestors. When the crypt was opened, we saw his mother's coffin buried in 1939 and his father's coffin buried in 1942 intact. In spite of this Mamuka asked us to bury her in real earth instead of the crypt when her time should come.

As a consequence of this sad event, our living space became larger. We had the room which used to serve as my father-in-law's harnessing workshop fixed up for Mamuka, and she gave up a room to our children. After a while she moved to an apartment in the house she and my father-in-law owned and rented out, because she wanted both children to have a room of their own. However, it soon turned out that she was unable to look after herself, so we brought her back.

She soon took to bed and did not want to get up any more. We could not persuade her even to take a little walk in the garden. A difficult year and a half ensued, the burden of which I would have gladly shared with my sister-in-law since I also had two children to look after, and I was sick again, this time with *struma* (goiter). Unfortunately, my sister-in-law was not willing to attend to Mamuka at all. We took Mamuka to their place in Khust only once after my *struma* operation, but my sister-in-law brought her back after one week. Allegedly she was longing after me! What could we do? We took good care of her ourselves. Poor Mamuka practically wasted away. Her weight dropped from seventy-three kilos to barely forty. Still when she died she did not have a wrinkle in her face or a single grey hair. We buried her in real earth in the Kapos Street cemetery close to our house.

In those months I was at home again unable to work because of my *struma*. According to my doctor my *struma* was provoked by excitement. I was so sick that even taking a loaf of bread home required a great effort of me, but fortunately an operation performed in May, 1957, cured me perfectly. In those years *struma* operations were done with local anesthesia. I spent two hours and forty minutes under the knife awake. The first days after the operation were very painful. Swallowing hurt very much. What is more, my doctor believed in my swallowing as often as possible, and he made me sip tea continually. He said I would recover faster that way. He was right. I was restored to health in a few days. I was particularly glad to see that the cut did not spoil my neck. It barely showed. Later it also became obvious that the operation was successful in a deeper sense: my heart complaints discontinued, and my pulse returned to normal.

It was not only because of my disease that I stopped working. I felt that if I wanted to raise my children properly it was not right to restrict the time I spent with them to the periods of the morning and evening rush. They needed more care both physically and spiritually. Both children brought very good grades from school and their behavior was also praised, therefore I did not notice for a long time that the two of them had struck a deal. Lia did the literature, composition, and drawing assignments for Öcsi—the subjects she was good at—and Öcsi did the mathematics and physics homework for Lia. By the time this became clear to me, they were already very much behind in the subjects which they left to the other one.

Actually, Lia was reliable when I worked full time. Öcsi, on the other hand, could be persuaded by friends to play truant. Lia never told us if her brother did not go to school. I still felt that something was wrong. I sensed the smell of cigarettes, even the smell of alcohol on Öcsi! I imagined what would become of him if he smoked and drank at that age already! Indeed, all his high school pals became alcoholics, three of them have even died already. These men, Öcsi's high school friends, all came from good families, only they were not interested in learning. Since Öcsi was very bright, it would have been a shame to let him waste his talents.

Under the influence of his pals, my son kept asserting that he would earn much better if he started working right after high school instead of studying. We tried to convince him that it was not only the momentary earnings that mattered. We insisted that first he should get a university degree, and then he could do whatever he wanted. In any case, it was clear that it was better for me to be on the alert and quit working. So I saw after the education of my children again, and it was worth it!

After I had recovered from *struma*, I had a chance to visit Czechoslovakia. My working place organized an excursion to the Tatra Mountains in Slovakia, and I combined it with seeing my relatives in Leles. First I went to see my second and third cousins, who welcomed me very kindly and also took me to see the distant relatives in other towns. Then I joined my colleagues with whom we visited the most beautiful sites of the Tatra range, including the Štrbské Pleso mountain lake. Finally, I went back to my relatives again for a few days, who showed me the city of Košice. That excursion is among the nicest experiences I have had in my life. It is also memorable because that was the first time I was allowed to leave the country in the Soviet era. Actually, it was not easy to arrange. I needed an invitation from my Czechoslovak relatives. Without an invitation one could not apply for a passport to leave. The passport looked like our ID, but we were not allowed to keep it. After returning from abroad we had to give it back to the authorities, and when we wanted to leave again we had to apply for it anew. We got back the same passport, but with a new entry in it. It specified for which days and where the passport was valid.

We also applied for permission to emigrate to the United States again. We received the answer that the children and I could go but Sanyi was not allowed to leave the country.

CHAPTER 21

On November 12, 1962 the women of our extended family were keeping vigil by Uncle Gyula Rehó's bier. In those days deceased persons were still laid out at home, and the night before their last journey the relatives and friends kept vigil by the body. The deceased was not a close relative. He was the husband of one of Sanyi's second cousins. Even so, I was overwhelmed with a great pain that I had never felt before. I fell into an uncontrollable fit of crying. "Father! Father!" I wailed, and I tumbled onto the coffin sobbing. I saw my father lying there. Since I could not calm down, I was taken home. The same thing happened the following day at the funeral. Only at the funeral feast could I regain my composure. We had no news from America until right before Christmas, when we were informed that my father had died on November 12th. I knew it! I had sensed it!

After Daddy's death Mommy decided she would try to come to see us. Naturally, it was impossible to come to the Soviet Union for a private visit. Only official tourists were let into the country, and they had to keep to an appointed route and a fixed timetable. They were accompanied by an appointed guide so that they would not even think of deviating from either the route or the timetable. Mommy arrived in Budapest, stayed with Katalin Bakos, Csöpike's sister, and began to arrange her "tourist trip." It took weeks to organize it. Uzhhorod was not designated as a city that could receive tourists, therefore it could not be entered by an American citizen. Mommy could choose between L'viv and Kiev. She chose L'viv because it was closer for both of us, and it was also closer to the West, which was reassuring to her. Mommy was given permission to spend five days in the Intourist Hotel in L'viv. The train which she had to take was also designated.

The Belgrade-Budapest-Moscow express spent three hours at the border town of Chop because the railway carriages had to be transferred with a crane onto the broad-gauge tracks used in the Soviet Union. The tourists were forbidden to leave the train during these three hours, including the time of the transfer. Some second- and third-class cars were also hooked onto the train at Chop for domestic passengers. These passengers were allowed to get into their cars only during the final ten minutes. Until then they could only peep at the train from behind the bars of the iron fence in front of the railway station. The place appointed as the location of our meeting was L'viv. We were not allowed to see each other at Chop. I wrote about this to Mommy. Nevertheless, we managed to meet at Chop already. They could not prevent us from doing so!

We caught sight of each other. After twenty-three years! Mommy was standing at the window of the train, and me, behind the bars of the. platform. The soldier kept pulling me back, shouting Nel'zia! Nel'zia! (It's forbidden, It's forbidden), but in vain! I did not care! We would not have minded even if they had shot at us! I broke through the gate of the iron fence, and Mommy jumped off the train, and we fell on each other's neck sobbing. Everybody could see that it was not an everyday encounter. In the end they did not disturb us. On the contrary, they let me, Sanyi, and Lia get into Mommy's international carriage. The conductor objected at first, but the soldier waved him to leave us alone, and Mommy also managed to calm him down with a few dollars. So we spent the six hours of the trip to L'viv across the Carpathian mountains all together, except for my son, who was away on an excursion to Estonia and Latvia, and was to join us later in L'viv.

At the L'viv railway station Mommy was met by her guide, a young Russian woman. She took us to the Hotel Intourist on Miczkiewicz Square in an elegant, chauffeured car. She was with us the whole time, including at meals at strictly fixed points of the day, and left Mommy alone only while Mommy was asleep. A friend of mine worked for Intourist, the Soviet tourist agency, and she warned me that Intourist hotels were full of microphones. Thus we talked inside the hotel conscious of the fact that the room was bugged. Mommy lived in a wing of the hotel that was reserved only for foreigners, and we lived in another one that was only for natives. We were glad to be allowed at least to live in the same building! That was only possible because Mommy paid in dollars for our rooms as well. Mommy later also managed to have her oldest grandchild be allowed to sleep in her room!

Mommy and I spoke only in English, so it must have been clear to the guide that no interpreting was necessary. In any case, she made us take part in all the obligatory touristic programs, and showed us all the sights of L'viv. They were actually new to me, too, because I had not seen them when I first went to L'viv following Sanyi in 1949. Öcsi arrived on the third day. That was the first time that Mommy had met her second grandchild. The five days fled as quickly as if they had been seconds. We applied for an extension of Mommy's visa, but our request was turned down, and the chauffeured car was soon back to take Mommy to the railway station. This time we could not manage to be allowed to join Mommy on the train, so we took an affectionate leave of each other. The Russian guide, however, gave us an idea! She took us to the domestic airport, where we boarded a little twenty-person airplane heading for Uzhhorod. We sat in the little old-fashioned, double-winged plane on long benches facing each other like in a tram. Over the Carpathians we fell into a turbulence so strong that the plane was jumping up and down. Nevertheless, we arrived safely in Uzhhorod, and took a train to Chop. Since it was a domestic train, we were allowed to get off, and we could wait for the Moscow-Budapest international express in the coffee shop of the Chop railway station. Mommy could again manage somehow to be let off the train, and we could spend another hour together. But it was not us who accompanied her back to her train but the soldier on duty. She spent still another month in Budapest, from where she telephoned every day. We waited for her call at the post office at four o'clock until her call came through.

In 1965 Mommy came to Budapest again and began to organize her Soviet tourist trip in the usual way. This time she was given permission to stay in Uzhhorod for a week, which was extended by three days. Naturally she was only allowed to stay in a hotel in Uzhhorod as well. After Mommy paid for one more person's accommodation, breakfast, and lunch in dollars, Lia was also allowed to join her in her hotel. We all gathered at lunchtime, dined together, and then visited our former favorite tourist sites.

Another unforgettable reunion also took place while Mommy was in Uzhhorod. Béla Moncsák, the son of our childhood landlady returned to Uzhhorod for the first time after the war. While he was still a student, a deep affection had evolved between him and my sister, Piru. He wanted to propose to her, and tried to emigrate to the United States but was not allowed to. He became an excellent internal medicine specialist in Uzhhorod and gave many injections to little Lia in the early forties. Poor Lia was very much afraid of injections, and Uncle Béla always managed to calm her down and comfort her with little presents. At the end of the war Béla got to Prague somehow, from where he tried to escape to the States. He was captured, then tortured and imprisoned. After being set free he became a doctor in a little town north of Prague. He never got married, but became a typical withdrawn bachelor. He was not allowed to visit his family until 1965 and he did not see his beloved sister, Incsu, for twenty years. He never got to see his parents again who had died in the meantime.

Poor Béla was inclined to depression, and Incsu, who was a university lecturer, could not be with him all the time because of the entrance examinations. Lia was already working, but she took a few days off to look after Béla. Incsu asked Lia not to leave him alone. They passed the time in the wonderful garden of the Moncsák villa, reminiscing about the past and talking about Piru.

We found it strange and suspicious that when we visited Béla he always received us deeply depressed, then disappeared in the bathroom and emerged in a much better mood. What we suspected turned out to be true: soon after he returned to Czechoslovakia he died of a morphine overdose.

Incsu Moncsák's fate was not less tragic. As a young woman she had married a Hungarian man in Budapest, but she remained in Uzhhorod—mainly because she could not leave her sick parents alone. By the time she was ready to join her husband, he died. Incsu nevertheless emigrated to Budapest as a widow. In the early seventies, she was once taking a walk near her apartment in Buda when a military vehicle knocked her down on the sidewalk and killed her.

Returning to Mommy, when the ten days allotted her in Uzhhorod were over, she went to see her remaining relatives in Leles, Košice, and Bratislava in Slovakia. Then she returned to her Budapest quarters with the Bakoses and waited for Lia. By then Lia had married a young Hungarian man from Dunaharaszti and was waiting for her permission to leave the country. The Moscow authorities were intent on delaying granting her permission to join her husband. By the time she was given her permit, her passport had expired, so the whole procedure had to be started anew. Mommy waited for her in Budapest, phoned to the Uzhhorod post office every day, and visited the new relatives in Dunaharaszti. Then she had enough of it and went back to America. Lia received her emigration papers right after Mommy's departure. Apparently, the authorities had been waiting for Mommy to return to America, and Lia was allowed to leave for Hungary only afterwards.

During the fifteen days we spent together with Mommy in 1963 and 1965 at last we learned everything about Daddy, my sister, and all the other members of my American family. Daddy worked for the Roebling's Sons Company until his retirement, earning very good wages. Soon after I had left they moved to Trenton, and they also bought a cottage at Seaside Heights. Unfortunately, Daddy suffered from arthritis, and his doctor recommended to him to move to a place with a warm, dry climate. So they sold their house in the late fifties and moved to Arizona. Daddy built a lovely home in Phoenix. Both Mommy and Daddy enjoyed the permanent summer of Arizona.

My sister got married soon after the war. During the war she was asked by an organization to correspond with an American soldier to keep his spirits up, and she and her penpal got so close that when the war was over, he went to see my sister first, rather than his family, and they soon got married. They had three sons. They stayed in New Jersey, but they heard such good things about Arizona from Mommy and Daddy that they followed them there. Mommy, who is now ninety-six years old, and my sister, who has become a widow, presently share a house with her youngest son in Phoenix. My sister attended college, became a teacher, and worked as a teacher in Trenton. In Arizona, on the other hand, she worked as a bookkeeper in a large furniture shop. Her husband became the manager of a supermarket.

Their eldest son, Robert, became an engineer, and his wife, Beverly, is a ceramic artist. Their only child, David, is an excellent athlete. For years he had only been interested in sports, but now he attends medical school. My sister's middle son, Richard, was an aviation specialist. He had a daughter from his second marriage. Unfortunately, Richard died of a heart attack at the age of forty-nine. My sister's youngest son, Ron, is a sports reporter. He is divorced with no children.

Mommy is confined to bed now. She had a spinal operation a few years ago. After the operation she could still move about very well with a cane, but then her condition began to deteriorate. First she had to use a walker, then she was not able to get up any more, but she has a clear mind to this very day.

I never returned to America after I left in 1938. Earlier the Soviet authorities did not let me go. Now we would be allowed to leave the country, but a trip to the United States is well beyond our means. Actually, I would hesitate to leave our home. If we left it here empty we would have nothing left by the time we returned. It seems I will never see Mommy again, and I will never return to the place of my happy youth.

CHAPTER 22

A fter missing a year because of her illness, Lia was able to study in Hungarian through the last exam of high school. In the upper classes teachers were less strict about the school uniform, so the girls began to look prettier. On holidays, for example, they were allowed to wear a dark skirt and a white blouse.

They studied mostly from good books, except for their history book, which was full of lies. I loved to take care of their books, doing things like preparing jackets for them. My love for beautiful, impeccable-looking books must have developed in the American elementary school where we did not buy the books, but merely borrowed them, and those who gave them back in good condition got special prizes. To this very day I have never taken a book into the kitchen or marked a page by folding up its corner. If a book that I lent to someone is given back to me stained or creased, I become very irritated.

My children had to work very hard in high school. An American student simply would not believe it. They had to sit for final exams in ten subjects. Lia was also asked by her teachers to help some weaker classmates prepare for the exam. Lia and these students studied night and day for weeks. They barely slept. I would ask them what they were doing at school all morning; why so much was left for home. Back in New Jersey we paid attention to what the teachers said, and never had to study anything at home, except perhaps for memorizing some poems. The afternoons and evenings were devoted to sports, games, the library, friendships, and the family.

Lia's main field of interest had always been drawing and painting, which she was not allowed to study because of her background. If she could not study art, she did not want to study anything at all. She looked for a job. She became a draftsman at a bridge-building company, then at an institute for agricultural architecture. Even so, she later attended a course at Uzhhorod University which qualified her to teach English in elementary school.

In the fifties and sixties it was in fashion to have penfriends. Young people collected and swapped the addresses of prospective penpals, recruiting their friends, too. Lia then got involved in an intensive, promising correspondence with a young man from Hungary who was a student at a military academy. He as good as proposed to Lia, and Lia also found him very attractive, handsome, and intelligent on the basis of his letters and photos, and she was seriously considering the possibility of leaving the country by marrying him. There was only one way for the penfriends to get acquainted in person: Lia had to take part in an organized tour to Hungary. The border could not be crossed privately in either direction. While Lia was waiting for the organized tour to take place, Mommy was staying in Budapest, and being a curious grandma she decided to visit the young man. It was during this meeting that he realized that Lia's grandmother was an American citizen. Having family in America was incompatible with an officer's career in the Hungarian army, so he wrote a beautiful, polite farewell letter to Lia. I hope he made a career for which it was worth giving up such a nice girl.

Even if not for the young officer's sake, Lia did take part in the tour to Hungary. The tour consisted of a four-day stay in Budapest and a four-day excursion to Lake Balaton. They had a very busy schedule which included not only sightseeing but also such ideologically motivated programs as "meeting with the Hungarian working youth," which meant in their case meeting with the builders of the Elisabeth bridge at a party. They barely had even a few hours off, although in fact every "tourist" went to Hungary to visit their relatives. Lia, too, planned to visit the two Demeter girls: Katalin Bakos, and Csöpike, who had already moved to Hungary by then.

As Lia was admiring the Parliament with her group, her bag opened and all her belongings dropped onto the stairs leading down to the Danube, but a handsome young man helped her collect her things. The following day when she was riding a tram on her way to the Bakoses, the very same young man greeted her on the tram, and accompanied her to the Bakos' house. On their last night in Budapest Csöpi and her husband organized a farewell party for Lia, where they wanted to introduce an eligible young man to her. To everybody's amazement, the young man—Miklós, an engineering student—greeted Lia as an old acquaintance. He was the young man who had helped Lia pick up her things at the bank of the Danube, and who had met her on the tram.

Miklós's sister worked together with Csöpike's mother-in-law, and it was their idea that Miklós should be introduced to Lia at a party. Lia actually felt after their two accidental encounters in a city with two million inhabitants that it was fate that decided they should meet. Lia and Miklós began to write to each other, and after a while they decided to get married.

The wedding took place in Uzhhorod on August 15, 1964. A church ceremony was out of the question, but we tried to make at least the civil ceremony held at the registrar's office memorable. Mommy promised to send a wedding dress with all the accessories from America. We were expecting the parcel to arrive any day, but we waited in vain, so at the last minute we had a pretty black dress with a white frill and white cuffs made for Lia. Then on the 13th of August we were notified that our parcel from America could be collected. Mommy sent a dream dress, and my Lia was a wonderful bride in it! Despite the simple civil ceremony a huge crowd gathered at the registrar's office. Apparently we were known and cared for by many.

The bridegroom's family could not attend the wedding. We were glad that the bridegroom himself was allowed to cross the border. We still had the nice big house in Kapos Street, so we had plenty of room for a wedding dinner. We invited the Magyar family and Lia's godparents: Cirill with his second wife, and Ilonka with her second husband. Lia and Miklós spent their honeymoon in L'viv. Then he went back to Hungary, and she remained and filled out an application to be allowed to leave the country to join her husband. She received permission to leave in May, but by that time her passport had expired, so she had to start the whole procedure all over again. Miklós wrote beautiful, romantic letters to her, and since he was a passionate photographer, he sent lots of photos of himself and his family. His father had been a subprefect in Dicsőszentmárton. After World War II, his county came under Romanian sovereignty, and he fled together with his wife and six children. They fled as far as Germany, but then they turned back, and a few years after the war they settled in Dunaharaszti, near Budapest, where he became a teacher.

Lia had to wait for more than a year, until September 12, 1965, to be allowed to emigrate. During this time Miklós managed to visit her only once. Lia finally arrived in Hungary with great expectations, hoping to become at last a citizen equal to all other citizens and to feel at last completely at home in her country. Not all of her expectations came true!

Lia joined Miklós in his parents' house in Dunaharaszti. Miklós's family received her kindly. Her mother-in-law was particularly glad to have someone to share the housework with. But Lia was disturbed by her total dependence on them and tried to find work as soon as possible. First she became an interpreter at the Central Statistical Office. She had to work an awful lot. At times she was sent for at night to correct some uninterpretable sentences in COMECON reports. Still it was not the work but her colleagues that disappointed her the most bitterly. They called her "Ruszki" (the nickname for Russians in Hungarian), and did not admit her to their company. It often happened that they sat down to have coffee and a chat, and left all the work to Lia, saying: "let the little Ruski do it!" What is more, Lia had to get up at 5 a.m. to get to the Statistical Office in downtown Budapest in time. So when she found out that ÉLGÉP, a company manufacturing machines for the food industry, was looking for a draftsman, she did not hesitate to apply. She was chosen from among the applicants in part because of her knowledge of languages. At ÉLGÉP Lia finally found what she was after. Her work was appreciated and paid well, and her colleagues also accepted her. Furthermore the company lay on the outskirts of Budapest in the direction of Dunaharaszti, which made life much easier for her. She needed that, because she was expecting a baby.

Although Lia was on good terms with her mother-in-law, her father-in-law proved to be an extremely rude person who created a constant tension in the house which Lia was not used to and could not bear. When she turned out to be pregnant, it also became obvious that Miklós was not prepared to take on the responsibility of a child. So Lia moved out. She rented a room in the house of the Kertész family whom she had gotten to know years before in Uzhhorod. They supported Lia and later her baby as well in every possible way. Lia's baby, Sándorka, was born on July 26, 1966. In those years Hungarian women were entitled to a six-month maternity leave, so when Sándorka was three weeks old, Lia got on the Budapest-Moscow express and came home to Uzhhorod. When the six months were over, Lia had the option of going back to Budapest with Sándorka and leaving him at a nursery fulltime, or leaving him with us. First she decided to leave him in our care, but after half a year she could not bear to be without Sándorka any longer. She managed to rent a room near ÉLGÉP and also found a nice nursery nearby, so she took the one-year-old Sándorka with her.

The arrangement worked out very well until one day the women at

ÉLGÉP received a phone call from the nursery that every child was sick, they had fevers and were vomiting. The women ran to collect their children, and to take them to their respective doctors. It turned out to be a very serious, chronic intestinal infection. Sándorka was sick for months until Lia found a specialist, a professor at the pediatric clinic, who was able to cure him. He said Lia must not take Sándorka back to the nursery. Lia, of course, was not in a position to stay at home with him. Sári Kertész, Lia's former landlady, offered to take care of Sándorka during the day, but I wanted Lia to bring him back to Uzhhorod. After all, we were his grandparents. We adored him, and he also loved us. I managed to convince Lia, so Sándorka came to live with us again. Lia's company had business relations with Uzhhorod, and they sent Lia on errands here every now and then, so we spent quite a lot of time together with her and made several nice excursions in the spring and summer of 1968.

On July 12th Sándorka said that he was not hungry. We thought of indigestion, but it was strange that the poor child did not want to drink, either. Our pediatrician was away on vacation in Odessa, so we called another pediatrician, and also asked a doctor friend of ours, Jóska Ujlaki, to examine him. They also diagnosed indigestion, but when he refused to eat and drink also the following day, they ordered him to be taken to the hospital. There he was given a transfusion, after which he ate a little, but threw up immediately. By the time they changed his bedclothes, poor Sándorka's forehead was hot, and a great turmoil started around us. "Mommy, tell me a story," Sándorka said to his mother, but by the time Lia could start the story, eleven doctors had surrounded Sándorka's bed. They put him on a stretcher, X-rayed him, and took him right into the operating room for a perforated appendix. The operation was performed by a very famous surgeon, Dr. Stepanian, who happened to be participating in a conference at the Uzhhorod hospital right then. Lia overheard the Russian doctors talking about peritonitis.

The operation lasted for two and a half hours. Our doctor friend came out pale. "We tried everything," he said. "The rest depends on the Lord." Sándorka died at two in the morning, on July 19, 1968. He was quietly lying in his bed, then he began fluttering his little hands higher and higher until he was gone. He would have been two years old on July 26th.

At five in the morning Elemér Ortutay, Lia's spiritual father, a Greek Catholic priest practicing his profession in secret, was already at our place. He hugged my daughter, and told her: "Be able to give away everything!" We buried Sándorka on July 21st, here in the Kapos Street cemetery. To this very day Lia visits Sándorka's grave first whenever she comes to Uzhhorod.

On the day of Sándorka's death a parcel arrived for him from Miklós, his father, with birthday presents: a toy car, a pair of trousers, and a pair of shoes. That was the first time that Miklós tried to contact Sándorka. They had never met. Fortunately, we gave Sándorka our birthday presents earlier, so he could still play with them for a while. Broken by grief, Lia first wanted to be away from Uzhhorod. She traveled to Khust and cried on the bank of the river Tisza. But she soon returned. She longed to be at Sándorka's grave in the Kapos Street cemetery.

One night Lia had a strange dream. As she told us, she saw Sándorka alive. He was swimming about in a beautiful blue lake, and she was looking at him with delight. Then there was a loud roaring of a motorcycle, and a colleague of Lia's appeared: Erzsike, together with her husband. "What a long way it has been!" she said. "Lia, please, go back to our daughter, and we will stay here with Sándorka," she added. Waking up from the beautiful, mysterious dream, Lia wrote to her boss to tell him what had happened and requested some days off. Her boss answered with a gentle, sympathetic letter, and also let her know that on July 22, the night of her dream, Erzsike and her husband had died, colliding front-on with another vehicle while riding their motorcycle.

It was the summer of 1968, and the socialist countries were preparing to invade Czechoslovakia. The Soviet troups in Subcarpathia were mobilized. Tanks and helicopters were rallying around Uzhhorod. Sanyi was afraid that the border would be sealed and urged Lia to go back to Hungary while it was still possible. Back in Budapest Lia sought solace in work and in the company of friends. She often visited the Kertész family, who had been Sándorka's godparents. Occasionally while there she met Sárika Kertész's nephew, Sándor, who tried to comfort her gently. Slowly mutual affection developed between them.

In 1969 Lia's company launched a house-building plan for its workers. Lia joined the plan. She saved carefully to be able to put down the advance payment required, but when her apartment was ready, it turned out that she was not eligible to buy it because she was not a Hungarian citizen. It took Lia years to get rid of her Soviet citizenship, then she was stateless for two years, and she received a Hungarian passport only after six more years, despite the fact that she was born a Hungarian citizen.

Dreams played an important role in the life of our family. So it happened again. My father appeared to Mommy in her dream and told her to set Lia's life right, that she should not continue adrift any longer. Mommy took this dream seriously, and wrote to Lia that if she found an appropriate apartment she would buy it for her. Lia was still not a Hungarian citizen, so she was still not entitled to own an apartment in Hungary, but when she revealed that the apartment would be paid for in dollars, all the obstacles disappeared. Lia found herself a nice apartment at the foot of the castle hill in Budapest, and she has been living there ever since. First she shared her apartment with a girlfriend of hers. Then in 1970 she married Sárika Kertész's nephew, Sándor. They got on very well together for several years, and had three nice children. In 1984, however, their marriage broke up.

Despite her divorces, Lia has managed to live a balanced, content life. She has handsome, good-natured, talented children. Zsolt, the oldest one, obtained a high school music teacher's diploma at the Budapest Academy of Music and is now studying organ playing there. Sándor, her second son, studied engineering and is now a novice in a monastic order. Edit, her daughter, attends college, and plans to be a teacher in a nursery school or a kindergarten. When after the collapse of the socialist system ÉLGÉP, Lia's company, was closed down, she went into early retirement, and since then she has been working as the sacristan of Saint Anna church.

CHAPTER 23

Öcsi had always been very good at all branches of natural sciences, but he had been best at chemistry. He not only knew chemistry very well, but also loved it, so it was obvious that he should become a chemist. After high school, however, he was not admitted to the chemistry department at Uzhhorod University because he did not pass the Ukrainian language exam. The language of teaching at Uzhhorod University was Russian, so it was actually not clear why he should be fluent in Ukrainian.

After his failure Öcsi found work in a nearby woodworking workshop preparing chess pieces, managed by our old friend Uncle Bertics. Öcsi liked to work with wood, but an accident broke off his career in woodworking. The lathe caught his index finger and hurt it so badly that the bone stuck out. After he recovered, he could neither fully straighten his finger nor fully bend it any more, as a consequence of which he was found unsuitable for regular military service. Fortunately, the Soviet Army did not want a conscript who was unable to pull the trigger properly.

When Öcsi failed in Ukrainian again and was not admitted to the chemistry department for the second time, he and his friend, Sándor Pricsni, decided to take the entrance examination for the Air Force Academy in Vyborg, near the Finnish border. Students who were admitted to the Academy had to sign a contract with the Air Force for twenty-five years. Our family was very much upset by Öcsi's decision, but still we did not want to interfere. Our principle was not to prevent our children from realizing their goals and desires. I was filled with anguish, but all I did was hope that Öcsi would not be admitted. His becoming a pilot would have meant for us a complete separation from him. The younger brother of a friend of mine, Kati Ujlaki, became an air force officer, and his family did not see him for twenty years. When he showed up again he was completely russified since he had been married to a Russian woman and had spent the previous twenty years of his life at Russian air bases from Kamchatka to the Kuril Islands. Fortunately Öcsi and his friend agreed that they would only enter the Air Force Academy together if both of them were admitted. Öcsi was accepted; his friend, however, was not! So the next problem for Öcsi to solve was to withdraw his application somehow, without any harmful consequences. He reported at the political commandership of the Academy and announced that he forgot to include certain facts in his biography, which, however, he did not want to hide from the commandership. Namely, he had an American grandmother, and a father with a criminal record. His name was immediately crossed off from the list of those admitted to the Academy without any comment. So both Öcsi and his friend could come home. We got our son back!

In 1959 Öcsi took the entrance examination at the chemistry department for the third time, but this time I also asked Irén Moncsák, who was a lecturer at Uzhhorod University, for help. She talked to her colleagues who tested the candidates in Ukrainian and managed to get Öcsi through. In the scientific tests Öcsi had the best scores of all. So he was admitted at last, and he studied chemistry for five years with excellent marks.

At the university, chemistry was mixed with ideological education, which, however, did not prove to be very effective in Öcsi's case. For example, students had to watch each other and to report if any one of them went to church. Öcsi was actually very glad when he was appointed for duty at some church to watch for students at the Sunday service, because then he could at last attend the service without any worries. On Monday, naturally, he reported that he had seen no students at the church at all.

In the Soviet Union the attitude of the State towards people with a university degree was that they had been educated at the expense of the State and consequently were entirely at the disposal of the State. As a matter of principle, people with a university degree were given jobs in republics or regions different from their place of origin. Such forced population exchange was an important element of the Soviet policy of assimilating national minorities. Non-Russian intellectuals spread in distant regions could not preserve their national identity. At the same time national minorities were deprived of their most conscientious, educated members, who came to be replaced by Russian professionals. The notion of temporary residence did not exist in the Soviet Union.

Once someone changed his passport valid in his place of origin for a passport valid in the place where he was appointed to work, there was no way for him to move back to his birthplace.

Öcsi was appointed to work in a chemical factory beyond the Ural mountains in Siberia, but he refused to accept the job. In the more relaxed atmosphere of the early sixties his diploma was not withdrawn for this (as would have happened before), but he was obliged to pay back the stipends that he received during his studies, and naturally he could not get a chemist's job in Subcarpathia. So he became a chemistry teacher in the high school of Shyshlivtsi (Sislóc). He soon obtained a teacher's diploma, as well. He merely had to pass some exams in pedagogy.

Öcsi continued his teacher's career at the high school in Chop. One of his students, Erzsébet (Zsike) Mitró, the daughter of the Protestant minister of the village of Solomonovo (Tiszasalamon), fascinated him so much that he married her after she finished high school. We held the civil wedding ceremony in Uzhhorod, and the wedding feast at Solomonovo. The day after the wedding Zsike's father also married the couple secretly in the Solomonovo church.

Öcsi and Zsike settled in Shyshlivtsi. Öcsi continued to teach at Chop, and Zsike became enrolled as a correspondence student at a college that trained nursery and kindergarten teachers in Mukachevo. In 1966 a daughter, Mónika, was born to them. They did not have an easy life, with Öcsi commuting and Zsike studying and taking care of a new baby in a house with no modern conveniences, so they decided to move in with us until Zsike finished her studies.

By that time our great house in Kapos Street had been expropriated, and we lived in a two-room apartment in an apartment building. When our house was taken away, we were promised two apartments in the same building instead: one for us, and one for Öcsi, who was also a grown-up at that time. Öcsi was to receive his apartment upon getting married. This promise was never fulfilled. Öcsi and his family had to share our two-room apartment where we lived together with Lia's son. They got our former bedroom, which was small, narrow, and hard to furnish, and which could be entered only from our room. The apartment was too small for anything but watching TV, and when Sanyi went to bed fairly early every evening, we could not even watch TV. So when Zsike got her diploma, they moved to Pallo (Palló), a Hungarian village near the Soviet-Slovak border. In villages it was not completely hopeless for young couples to obtain a house or apartment of their own. Zsike's brother was married to a Hungarian citizen, and lived in the city of Debrecen in Hungary. He was active in the Hungarian Patriotic People's Front, an umbrella organization dominated by the Communist Party, and had many useful connections. In 1972 he sent an official invitation to Öcsi, Zsike, and their daughter, declaring that he and his wife would provide for them, and would also put an apartment at their disposal. This was sufficient for Öcsi and his family to be allowed to move to Hungary. In fact, Zsike's brother and his wife were to share their own apartment with the three of them. However, it turned out within days after their arrival in Hungary that a new school and nursery was to be opened in Kaba, a town near Debrecen, and the local council was looking for teachers and also offering apartments for them. Öcsi and Zsike applied, and Öcsi came to be employed as a Russian teacher and Zsike as a kindergarten teacher. This happened so fast that they were able to transport their furniture packed up in Pallo directly to their new apartment in Kaba. Their daughter, Monika, was six years old at that time, so she could begin school in Hungary.

Öcsi and Zsike have been living happily in Kaba ever since. When Zsike's father died, her mother also moved in with them. She sold her house in Solomonovo, and with the help of the money she received for it they had a nice house built in Kaba. Öcsi has become an all-round teacher who has taught not only Russian and natural sciences, but also English, and now he is the vice principal of his school. Zsike obtained a further degree in Budapest and has become the head of the Kaba nursery and kindergarten. She is famous in the whole region for arranging theater and dance performances with the kids. The costumes and other accessories for the performances are prepared by her mother, who is well known for her work in sewing and crafts.

In the meantime Monika also grew up and got married to the son of my friend Alizé Teke. They live with their two children, Péter and Helga, in Tiszalök, Hungary. I meet my friend Alize every so often, and it is a great pleasure for both of us that her grandchildren are my great-grandchildren.

CHAPTER 24

I n 1966, we were ordered to leave the ancestral house of the Laszota family, because the area was to be reconstructed. They planned to build a five-storey apartment building and a restaurant on the site. We did not attempt to resist because Lia's son, Sándorka, was staying with us, and we did not want to risk having the water and electricity turned off. We could choose between two two-room apartments as a compensation. Both were in the same apartment building, one on the third floor looking northeast, and one on the fourth floor looking southwest. We chose the third-floor apartment and began to move. The first day we took along only as much furniture as we were able to. When the next morning we went back to our Kapos Street house for the rest, several of our belongings had already been stolen! Our garden had been robbed of everything in one night! The kohlrabis had been pulled out of the ground, our wonderful vines had been uprooted. The cherries had been stolen together with the tree. The tree had been simply cut off above the ground. When Sanyi got to the house, one of our neighbors was just removing Sanyi's tools from their wooden box. When Sanyi asked him what he was doing there, he hemmed and hawed that he thought those things were not wanted by anybody. But we had not moved out yet! That was what the world around us had turned into under the Soviet system!

The old Kapos Street was demolished. Today it is lined by five-storey blocks of apartments. Only three townhouses were left on the other side of the street as mementoes of what the former middle-class Uzhhorod had been like. Of the old Uzhhorod basically only the public buildings erected in the Czechoslovak era have survived, as well as the Galago, a section built for the civil servants of the Czechoslovak administration. These buildings are still of incomparably better quality than anything built since then.

The Kapos Street cemetery, where Mamuka was laid to rest in 1962, still exists, but it is in horrible condition. The beautiful, vaulted monuments have been demolished, the wooden crosses have been burnt, everything has been destroyed. Nobody has been buried there for a long time, and it has become the gathering place of robbers and knaves. People do not dare to visit the graves of their dead relatives any longer because even murders have occurred there. The city management wants to establish a park in its place, and has called upon the descendants of the dead to have the remains of their relatives transferred to the Way of the Cross cemetery. Many of our acquaintances have done so, but we have decided to let Mamuka rest. We know where she lies, and we will continue to visit her grave regularly, to take her flowers, and to light a candle for her on her birthday, at Christmas, and on All Soul's Day no matter what happens to the cemetery around her. When we are gone, there will be no one left to visit her grave any more. We have no relatives left in Uzhhorod.

When Sanyi was approaching retirement, a friend of his offered him a much better paid job than what he had. Since the amount of a person's pension depended in part on his monthly income in the period prior to his retirement, Sanyi took the offer. He had to track down people who bought furniture on the rent-to-own plan and who disappeared without paying the installments. It was quite common that people who were about to move to distant republics bought things on this plan with the intention of never paying the full price. My Sanyi was just as meticulous and persevering in his new job as he had been in everything else and he proved to be extremely successful as well. He managed to recover sums which nobody counted on any more. He also liked his work, mainly because it involved a lot of travel. He retired in 1972, at the age of sixty, but he worked for two more years as a pensioner.

After both of us became pensioners, Lia wanted us to join her in Hungary, but our applications for emigration were turned down. Until 1985 even permission to visit our children was hard to come by. The local authorities invariably refused our applications. We had to appeal repeatedly to higher and higher authorities, which took months.

When Gorbachev came to power in 1985, travel abroad became possible. We could also speak freely, newspapers could write the truth, and in general people were relieved. At the same time there was no anarchy yet because the army and the police were still functioning. We felt both free and safe.

In 1991, Ukraine became an independent state, the ruble ceased to be its official currency, and we lost all our savings. We had 4000 rubles in the bank, our life's savings. It was a large sum, the price of a new Lada. We had been putting it together little by little so as to have safety reserves for our old age. When Sanyi became a pensioner but went on working, we saved his pension and lived on what he earned. I made extra money by embroidering blouses and saved at least 50 rubles of my earnings every month. When Ukraine became independent, we were informed by our bank that our 4000 rubles were changed into eight million Ukrainian coupons. It meant we practically lost all we had. Eight million coupons would not be enough even for a burial, as a coffin costs eighteen million, and the funeral fifty million. But we could not keep even our eight million coupons. They were changed into shares, which are not worth as much as a few pounds of flour.

In 1990-1991 Sanyi was rehabilitated. He was at first given 3000 rubles, then 10,000 rubles, and eventually 188,000 rubles in compensation for the six years he had spent in prison camp. We immediately changed the money into Hungarian currency. We received 6000 forints for it, at that time roughly the equivalent of fifty US dollars. Sanyi was also given twenty pounds of flour, a pair of shoes, and a free train pass valid within fifty kilometers (thirty miles) around Uzhhorod. Unfortunately, Khust, where we go regularly to visit his sister, is one hundred thirty kilometers away. The most important element of the compensation has been the so-called 50% rebate: Sanyi has to pay only fifty percent of rent and utilities until the end of his life. We are very lucky to have this rebate because without it we could not make ends meet.

We pay a flat rate for central heating for twelve months a year. Despite the fifty percent rebate it costs us 766,000 rubles. The heating should in principle begin on October 15th, but it never starts before Christmas. At Christmas we receive a little heat at last, but the corroded pipelines cannot stand the pressure, the system breaks down, and then there is no heating for a week. And it goes on like that for the whole winter. We get a little heating for two days, then nothing for a week. Last winter the temperature was regularly around 8° centigrade (about 45° Fahrenheit) in our apartment. We got some heat by having the gas-cooker on in the kitchen, or by turning on a small electric radiator. However, if the radiator is turned on, no other electric appliances can be used because the fuse would melt.

The power supply is also catastrophic, especially in the winter. Uzhhorod is divided into five zones. The first one gets no electricity on

Monday after four p.m., the second one on Tuesday, and so on. We have no electricity on Friday. We are prepared for that. We have candles at hand, we empty the refrigerator in advance, and we plan no activity that would involve the use of electricity.

Everything around us is run down. The staircase of our apartment building is dirty, ruined, and has been robbed of all that is worth anything. It looks worse than a stable. Since the lightbulbs were immediately unscrewed and snatched away both in the staircase and in front of the house, our caretaker had fifteen bulbs with a wire-mesh cover installed. All of them were stolen the first night. The next morning only some torn wires stuck out of the wall. Perhaps it was the robbers burglarizing the apartment above us three days later who had made sure that the staircase was pitch dark. The apartment above us was ransacked so thoroughly that even the faucets and lamps were torn out; only the bare walls remained.

Since Ukraine became an independent state, there has been complete anarchy. In the Soviet times huge factories were established here, among them a motor factory, a dynamo factory, a factory manufacturing precision instruments, and a shipyard. Each of these factories employed three to five thousand workers, mainly Russians recruited from far away regions of the Soviet Union. The factories do not work anymore, or if they do, they do not pay their workers. Practically everybody is out of work. Some try to find work in the private sector, where wages are paid in dollars. Others buy and sell, and still others cheat, steal, and pillage. After all, people have to eat!

A tiny fraction of the population has become very rich. Now the city's shops are full of goods again, and they sell everything just like before the war, except that this time very few people can afford to shop in them. New banks have opened, more and more Ukrainian-Hungarian, Ukrainian-Slovak, Ukrainian-Polish companies have begun to operate. However, most Uzhhorod citizens do not benefit at all from this. What we experience is that our pensions are worth only a third of what they were before.

The other day Sanyi met a Russian acquaintance of his and was complaining to him about the situation. His answer was: "We have potatoes, we have salted herring, we have vodka. What else do you need?" With such unambitious people it will be hard to make any progress.

A positive change as compared to the Soviet times has been that we are not forced to lie about our national identity any longer. This does not hold of the Rusyns, whose existence is still denied. They are still called Ukrainians. As for us, during the Soviet era we were regarded as Slovaks, but now we are recorded as Hungarians. Sanyi actually still has his ID issued by the Hungarian authorities in 1939 testifying to his Hungarian citizenship. I, on the other hand, must still be an American citizen, as I have never renounced my citizenship.

Incidentally, a while ago I had six visitors from New Jersey. I apologized for my rusty English, and explained to them that I had not used my mother tongue for sixty years. When saying good-bye to me they said I could speak Engish as if I had never left America. It would have been good if I could have earned my living by teaching English or translating, but I did not learn Ukrainian and Russian well enough. I still regret that my sister-in-law did not allow me to take Ukrainian lessons when I was seventeen. Later I could not afford to devote my energies to learning languages any more since I was struggling to ensure our day to day survival.

Today we live a very tranquil life. We get up at six in the morning. While I prepare breakfast, Sanyi heats water for us to wash and makes the beds. After breakfast he might help me a little bit in the kitchen, then at half past nine he visits his doctor, Kati Ujlaki. If he fails to show up in her consulting room for some reason, Kati comes to see us in the afternoon. After visiting his doctor, Sanyi goes to the grocer's and to the market, while I prepare dinner. We eat dinner at noon, then we have a short nap. In the afternoon we do the remaining chores around the house, then we read, or I knit. Sanyi's favorite reading is *Life and Science*, a popular scientific journal. He has every volume of it. At six o'clock we turn on the TV, and watch the Hungarian Television program. We watch the news, quizzes, and films. Then we go to bed.

We still regularly see some of our friends, first of all Aliz Teke, the mother-in-law of my granddaughter, and Rózsika, Aunt Olga's daughter, who has been widowed by now, but our former social life has ceased. The Hungarian citizenry of Uzhhorod has almost disappeared, and literally nobody has remained of our generation; they have either died or emigrated. Most recently it was Lajcsi Koppelmann, Sanyi's classmate of eight years and good friend of eighty years, who moved to St. Petersburg, where his daughter is a concert violinist. He has to begin his life anew in his eighties; may God help him! Of our two shoemaker acquaintances, Mr. Moskowitz emigrated to Israel at the age of eighty, and Mr. Levkowitz emigrated to the United States at the age of eighty-four. My former friends are also spread around the world. We had a reunion a few years ago in Uzhhorod. Kati came from Budapest, Zsuzsi from New York, Edit Klein from Israel.

My sister-in-law, Ilonka, is eighty-six years old. We visit her in Khust every summer and also correspond with her regularly. If we do not hear from her for two weeks, we phone her. When she became widowed a few years ago, she signed a contract with a young Ukrainian couple. They paid her a certain sum and undertook to take care of her until the end of her life, and in return she named them as her heirs. Of the amount she received from them she also gave us some money—naturally in dollars—in compensation for her old debt. She has never repaid the seven thousand dollars. What she gave us from the price of her house was also symbolic. Still, I am not as angry with her because of that as my parents used to be. None of us here were in control of what happened to us; neither was she. And my American family could part with that money without difficulty.

The young Ukrainian woman looking after my sister-in-law takes good care of her. It is only her way of cooking that Ilonka does not like. She cooks in the Ukrainian style, using plenty of cabbage, beetroot, tomatoes, garlic, and spices completely different from what we are used to. So my sister-in-law, who has always been an excellent cook, prefers to do her own cooking. Having a home and a caretaker, and having no children, she can afford to spoil herself with the little pension she gets.

Our subsistence is based on the two pensions we receive, Sanyi's fifty percent rebate, and the support of our children, primarily that of Lia. Whereas our neighbors practically starve, thanks to Lia we have enough even to put some aside. At this moment our larder contains twenty-five pounds of flour, seven pounds of lard (that is what Hungarians cook with instead of oil), forty-five pounds of sugar, ten pounds of coffee, three packages of tea, thirty boxes of matches, and various spices.

A while ago we renewed our application to join our daughter in Hungary. We do not really want to leave Uzhhorod, but we are getting old, we have less and less time left. If either of us passes away, the other one cannot survive alone and will not be safe. We need the emigration permit for that point in time when one of us ends up in the family crypt in the Way of the Cross cemetery, so that the other one can join our children right away.

That has been the story of my life. I grew up in a wonderful, affectionate, harmonious family. I was surrounded by beauty, comfort, and prosperity in America. Only love was able to entice me from there! It is important to add that when I left America for Sándor Laszota, Uzhhorod was also part of the same world, providing possibilities for a similarly beautiful, smooth, harmonious middle-class life. If I had known in advance how history was going to treat us, I probably would never have left. I did not foresee the future, and I lived through all the horror inflicted upon us. Still, despite everything, I can say I have never regretted my decision for a moment. My Sanyi and I have been living in marvellous love and affection to this very day. We have never quarrelled, nor have we ever said even a loud word to each other. We have raised our children to be honest, respectable adults, and we can be proud of our grandchildren and great-grandchildren, too. My family has always held together. We have helped and protected each other in all circumstances.

In America my lot could have been easier. I could have led a prosperous, balanced life without any shocks. Probably I would also have spent my old age in greater financial, legal, and physical safety. To be a little ironic, in Subcarpathia, on the other hand, I have never been bored. I was tested: Could I hold out in difficult, often hopeless situations? Could I manage a family and hold it together in times when everything was working against us? Were my morals firm enough in an immoral world? Could I bring up my children to be faithful and honest in an environment which was faithless and which punished honesty? Could I remain loyal to my friends in various historical catastrophes? Could I preserve love in my heart amidst war, prison, poverty, and years of loneliness? If I had lived a pleasant middle-class American life, I would never have known what qualities and how much strength I have. Naturally, I do not mean to say that I approve of people being subjected to such trials.

I also owe it to Uzhhorod and to the terrible historical, political, financial, moral, and health situations we have gone through here that I have learned how many good, strong, and honest people there are. I owe thanks to many friends, acquaintances, and unknown persons for giving us lodging when we had no place to go; for sending us milk in the mornings when the children needed it the most; for forwarding Sanyi's letters to us, thereby keeping alive the hope in all of us. As an American housewife I would certainly have had much less experience with these human qualities.

Now that I am old, of course, I would not mind a somewhat more secure life, but perhaps if I had remained at home in America I would not even have lived to be old. If I had stayed, I might have been hit by a car in New York fifty years ago. Who knows? Mommy said a long time ago, when we were caught in the storm at sea: "God gave it; it will be the way He wants it."

Amen.

Mary Halász
Uzhhorod
January 1997

Photographs

1. Mary as a young teenager in Hungarian costume, in front of the family house in Roebling, New Jersey.

2. Mary (left) with her father and sister on their street in Roebling, New Jersey.

3. Mary (left) with her mother and sister on the ocean crossing to Europe, 1934.

4. The last time together as a family, Roebling, New Jersey, 1937.

5. Mary's family back in America with their first car, 1941.

6. *Mary's fiancée to-be, Sándor Laszota in 1934, the photo her friends thought to be that of a European film star.*

7. *Sándor, the teacher, with his students from the Czechoslovak Army, with a photo of Mary, his fiancée, 1938 .*

8. *Mary and Sándor on the promenade in Uzhhorod, 1938, during their long engagement.*

9. *Mary and Sándor on their wedding day, July 3, 1938.*

173

10. The young and happy couple.

11. Mary's sister-in-law Ilonka and her mother, Uzhhorod, 1938.

174

12. Mary (right) with Ilonka, Sándor, and daughter Lia, Uzhhorod 1940.

14.Mary's father-in-law with her son Öcsi and daughter Lia, 1942.

13. A family photograph from 1941, before Sándor was called up by the Hungarian Army.

15. *Mary dressed as young Rusyn wife in the village of Turia Bystra, Subcarpathian Rus'.*

17. *Proud father Sándor holding son in the yard of the home in Turia Bystra.*

16. *Nenuka, the family's Rusyn maid, dressed for Sunday mass in Turia Bystra.*

176

18. Family photograph taken for the American passport that was stolen during the train ride from Moscow to Uzhhorod.

19. Mary's children, Lia and Öcsi, in the garden of their house in Uzhhorod, ca. 1949.

20. One of the many Christmases during Soviet times, celebrated in secret, behind closed curtains.

21. *Mary and her best friend and chief support, Csöpike Demeter, on the bank of the Uzh River.*

22. *Mary at a women's party at the Demeters' house, her friends Csöpike and Aliz Teke, among others, Uzhhorod, ca. 1952.*

23. Sándor soon after his return to Uzhhorod from the Gulag, with Mary, her mother-in-law (left), the children Öcsi and Lia.

24. After two decades, Mary and her family finally meet her mother in the company of a Soviet guide on the left, L'viv 1962.

25. *Mary and her mother (left) meeting for the last time with Irén and Béla Moncsák,
Uzhhorod 1964.*

26. *Family portrait at Lia's wedding in front of the embroidered coat-of-arms of the
Soviet Union, Uzhhorod 1964.*

180

27. Mary's son Öcsi on his wedding day with Zsike. Zsike is wearing the same American dream dress that in 1938 Mary's mother had sent her, Uzhhorod 1965.

28. Mary's daughter Lia, with her son Sándorka shortly before his death, Uzhhorod 1967.

29. After 44 years, Mary (left) and Sándor meet her sister Piru, Budapest 1981.

30. Mary and her grandchildren in the early 1980s.

31. *The shop of Mary's brother-in-law, Cirill Fundanics, survives the Soviet era, Uzhhorod 1998.*